RIGHTS OF LIGHT
and how to deal with them

RIGHTS OF LIGHT and how to deal with them

John Anstey
BA FRICS FCIArb

R·I·C·S BOOKS

for
The Royal Institution of Chartered Surveyors
12 Great George Street, London SW1P 3AD

Published on behalf of
The Royal Institution of Chartered Surveyors
by RICS Books
12 Great George Street, London SW1P 3AD

Scottish Branch Office
7 Manor Place, Edinburgh EH3 7DN

First edition November 1988

ISBN 0 85406 551 2

Illustrations by Michael Cromar

Typeset by Columns of Reading
Printed in Great Britain by Blackfords of Cornwall

Contents

Introduction

My late father, Bryan Anstey, was already well known as a rights of light consultant when he persuaded me to specialise in party walls. He was of the opinion that although the two matters often both needed dealing with at the same time, it was better to have them dealt with separately, since one was a common law affair and the other was statutory. For some years, therefore, we carried on the practice of those two specialities side by side and when, in 1974, he handed over the rights of light to me, I passed the party walls into the care of Mike Bailey who was then my right-hand man in such matters. Nowadays I have a partner, Lance Harris, to do all the hard work.

Using the knowledge of the law and practice of party wall procedure that I had gained over the preceding twenty-odd years I wrote *Party Walls and what to do with them*, which was intended to be a practical handbook to the subject. I had originally intended to follow that with a revised and up-to-date edition of my father's book entitled *The Right to Light*, but when I was unable to agree with the publishers on just how that was to be done, I decided with the enthusiastic support of Surveyors Publications to write a companion volume to my own work on party walls, and this is it.

I have scrupulously avoided reading *The Right to Light* since I started on this project, so that what follows is my own unaided work, except that it is bound to be the product of the advice and counsel I received for years from my father, and am still receiving from Michael Cromar, and opponents like Keith McDonald, Eric Roe and Michael Pitts. I have a feeling, which I won't be able to check until I have finished this book, that it is a more practically slanted handbook than my father's, and certainly it has not had the benefit of a distinguished lawyer to check my views of the law – which my father had in the late Michael Chavasse QC. As audiences of my written and spoken works elsewhere will know, I tend to be rather opinionated, and so as well as the formal disclaimer which the publishers will print at the front of this book, I would add my own words of warning here. Although I have always given my view of the law as carefully as I can, and made it clear when I am expressing an opinion, you would be extremely foolish to rush off to court without taking careful legal and professional advice about your particular case. No book, and certainly not one which is meant to be a readable guide, can cover every eventuality, while the law frequently changes as new cases move it in one direction or another. Just look at the law on professional liability, which seems never to be the same for two successive cases.

Don't throw away my father's book if you've got it, and borrow it from a library if you haven't: it's now out of print. Buy a copy of *Gale on Easements* (Sweet and Maxwell) for the best guidance I know on the general law on the subject: but don't forget what the Court of Appeal said to the County Court Judge in *Pugh* v *Howells* (which see). An excellent technical book on daylight is *Principles of Natural Lighting* by J.A. Lynes. This, too, may be out of print, but it's worth keeping an eye open for a copy. And then you're still going to have to use your skill and your judgment.

When you are involved in rights of light cases, look for agreements. Ask the client, the solicitors and the architects if they know of any; and then ask again. Even as I write these words, an agreement has turned up which may revolutionise a major development, although the job has been under way for over a year on the assumption that no such agreement existed. Look at the buildings involved to decide how old they are. Ask the local authority, both rating and building control departments. Seek out any alterations, and look closely. On one of the very first jobs my father allowed me to tackle alone, I was thoroughly deceived by a window which had been moved complete with its surround, and so carefully married to the brickwork around it that I was convinced that it was coeval with the nineteenth-century building which housed it. (Fortunately, my opponents had made an even more drastic mistake in their proceedings, and a grateful client took me out to supper: that doesn't happen too often.)

Don't, unless it's absolutely necessary, and then only with caveats as long as the original contract in *A Night at the Opera*, try to assess a rights of light situation on the basis of other people's drawings and photographs. They may have failed to draw or photograph the very item – a distant building, an alternative source of light – which swings the whole case.

Do try to be positive in your advice. Of course you must make it clear when you cannot give an absolutely certain reply. As will become clear to you later in the book, you can never be sure about injunctions and sometimes not even about whether an injury is actionable, let alone nice points of law but, as far as is consistent with those uncertainties, be as clear and straightforward as you can in your advice, and don't render it useless with a whole bunch of ifs and buts.

If you can't give advice without looking over your shoulder for a possible negligence claim, don't take the job. I always imagine that I carry no insurance, so that I have to make absolutely sure that the advice I give is correct, and then that I am insured to the hilt against any disaster, so that I can give my advice boldly and without fear of any adverse consequences to myself.

I am never more pleased than when I receive a letter thanking me for my succinct and straightforward advice. If this book helps you to provide the same service to your clients – or if you feel that it has done so for you – I shall be well pleased indeed.

Chapter 1

What is a right to light?

A right to light is an easement: that is to say, it is a right acquired by one party (the dominant owner) over someone else's land. This latter person is called the servient owner. There are surprisingly few natural rights in English law, and many people are mistakenly under the impression that certain rights do exist which don't. There are, contrariwise, a surprising number of rights which can be acquired – and some of the rights are themselves surprising. For example, you can acquire a right to mix muck on a neighbour's land, or project your bowsprit over his land. It is certain that the list of easements known to the law is not closed.

This leads me back to the consideration of 'what is an easement?' The characteristics of an easement were set out in a case as recent as 1956, known as *re Ellenborough Park*. They are:

1. there must be a dominant and a servient tenement;
2. an easement must accommodate the dominant tenement;
3. dominant and servient owners must be different persons, and
4. a right over land cannot amount to an easement, unless it is capable of forming the subject matter of a grant.

You can find a very detailed examination of these four characteristics in *Gale on Easements*, a magnificent legal textbook. I own three editions: the thirteenth, heavily annotated by my father; the fourteenth, heavily thumbed by me; and the fifteenth, which I haven't had time to do more than glance at so far. *A propos* of the fourteenth, I must tell you a favourite anecdote of mine. I was attending a conference with counsel, and had propounded a certain view of the law. Counsel asked where I had got that idea from, and I replied: 'From *Gale*'. He took a well-worn copy from his bookshelf, and started to flick through it, but I took it from him, saying that I could probably find the passage quicker than he. I did so, and handed it back to him. He read the page and said: 'Well I know I put my name to this volume, but . . .' I don't know who was more embarrassed, he because I had to point it out to him, or I for not knowing that he was one of the editors. For the study of easements in general, and rights of light in particular, I find *Gale* eminently readable and full of interesting matter.

For our purposes, I think that the most important qualities of an easement are the last two, and I shall spend a little time on them. In a way, the third is the same as the first, but not quite. The easiest way to examine this question is by considering rights of way over Whiteacre and Blackacre. If the same chap owns both, then when he walks from Blackacre on to Whiteacre he does so not because he has the right to do so as the owner of Blackacre, but as the owner of Whiteacre. If someone else owns Whiteacre, and yet the owner of Blackacre habitually walks across the former's land – perhaps because it is a useful short cut – then he may in time acquire a right to do so, even if the owner of Whiteacre wants to stop him. (We will look at the question of acquisition a little later.) It is quite clear, therefore, that there must be two separate owners: that there must be two separate tenements seems to me self-evident, but there it is – or they are.

There is one interesting side point here. Whereas in the case of most easements a tenant cannot prescribe against his landlord, he can do so for light. Normally, any 'rights' which he enjoys are held through the right of his landlord and since, see above, you've got to have two different people, he can't have an easement in the right of his landlord over his landlord's other property – except, I repeat, in the case of light.

The fourth characteristic, capability of being the subject of a grant, means that the right must be a clearly defined one, which could be put into words and made binding on the servient tenement. This is a lot easier to do with positive easements, such as the two I have already cited (or with some of the other more amusing ones, such as the right to hang clothes lines over a neighbour's land, or to use his kitchen to do your washing) than with negative easements, which is what a right to light is. It is not a right for you to do something but a right to stop your neighbour from doing something himself on his own land. It has been argued that this is not capable of forming the subject matter of a grant – and in *Dalton* v *Angus*, 1881, it was even contended that support was in a similar category. Fortunately for us – and especially for me – it seems now to be established beyond question that a right to light is an easement, so we needn't enter into recondite legal arguments.

It is not, strictly speaking, relevant to this book, but you may care to think about whether the requirements could be satisfied for a fire escape. There is no easement recognised as yet to a fire escape, because it is argued that unless you run up and down the fire escape, you're not using it in a way that establishes your right. I maintain that, in circumstances which dictate that you must have a fire escape in order to be allowed to occupy an office at all, you 'use' the fire escape simply by sitting there. The time will come, mark my words, when the existence of a fire escape will matter so much to someone that they will bring a successful action to prove that you can enjoy a right by inertia.

There is no easement to a view or to sunlight. That is a bald statement which you will find in every formal rights of light report that I make, and which certainly needs driving home. In fact, very often it is view or sunlight which looms much larger than daylight in people's minds in objecting to a development proposal, certainly in domestic cases. Funnily enough, in view of what I've said about grants, you can have a right to a view, but not an easement. Early in the 1980s there was a case in which someone in Cornwall had sold some land between his house and the coast, with an express reservation that no building should be constructed which obstructed the view. The court of first instance awarded damages against an offending building, but the Court of Appeal gave a mandatory injunction. (These various remedies will be dealt with in a later chapter.) However, a view is generally too lacking in the ability to be defined for it to be the subject of an easement.

Sunlight is a different matter. My father used to say that, in England, the incidence of sunlight was far too uncertain for the law to interest itself in the matter, but that was before the days of solar panels. It is my opinion that since the incidence is so uncertain, and since solar panels need every scrap of sunlight which parsimonious Nature throws to them, the intrusion of a substantial obstruction to that sunlight may lead someone who has spent a small fortune on his solar installation to risk a still larger fortune on establishing a new right, even though it will be in the more difficult second division of negative easements. For the time being, however, it is only the planners who may need to be satisfied about sunlight (and I shall be looking at them a little later), not the courts.

Well, here we are, 1,500 or so words into this chapter, and I haven't really told you what a right to light is, except that it is an easement. Once again, it may be easier to start by saying what it is not. It is not a right to receive the same light for ever, or to have no obstruction of any kind. It is a right to be left with 'a residual quantum adequate according to the ordinary notions of mankind'. Or, to put it another way, to be left with 'enough'. I am sure that my first definition comes from a judgment, though I can't find it, but there are several which I can find which say much the same. In *Colls* v *Home and Colonial Stores*, 1904, Lord Lindley said that a dominant owner was entitled to 'sufficient light according to the ordinary notions of mankind for the comfortable use and enjoyment of his house as a dwelling house', while Lord Davey said that he had a right to enough 'for the ordinary purposes of inhabitancy or business of the tenement according to the ordinary notions of mankind'.

What, then, are the ordinary notions of mankind? Well, it is my opinion that they are, in law, a good deal less than the man on the Clapham omnibus thinks that they are. I know that that is a contradiction in terms, but let me explain a little further. I intend to write a whole chapter about the measurement of light, so I will only give a vague outline of the technicalities here.

It was for many years held to be a good working rule that, if a room was left with half its area, at the working plane, lit to a certain minimal standard, then that room, however much light it had lost, was not injured. That minimal standard was one lumen, the equivalent of the light from a standard candle at one foot distance. This, the so-called 50/50 rule, was upset by *Ough* v *King*, 1967, but no other standard was substituted. Since, as Solon said, it is better for the law to be certain than for it to be just, this has led to an unfortunate uncertainty, since no-one – not even the most wise, experienced and skilful consultant, such as your present writer – can advice an owner with absolute certainty as to his position.

Nevertheless, the 50/50 rule remains a good general guide, and most practitioners use it most of the time. They add a word of caution, however, especially to people involved in domestic cases, if the area remaining well lit is in the 50% to 55% area.

The incidence of light at the working plane is measured by referring to the amount of sky which can be seen from the spot and, as will be explained later, this can be related to the one lumen standard.

I can sum up this chapter by saying that a right to light is an easement; that the right is to have daylight available from the sky; that you are entitled only to be left with adequacy, not more; and that adequacy is something like half the room well lit at table level.

Chapter 2

How to acquire a right to light

Since it is an essential characteristic of an easement that it should be capable of forming the subject matter of a grant, it must follow that you can acquire a right to light by express grant. An express grant is just what it says: a formal document (or part of one) in which one party specifically grants the other a right to receive light to certain windows. An express reservation is like unto it, and is definitely part of some other document, usually a contract for sale. The vendor reserves to himself a right of light to certain windows in the building he is retaining, thus effectively stopping the purchaser from constructing whatever takes his fancy on his new site. Since, you will doubtless remember, you cannot have a right of light over your own land, those windows would not otherwise have any rights over land which the vendor was selling off out of his holding.

In many ways, express grants (and for grant, read also reservation in this context) are the most difficult to deal with, because they can be expressed in such vague and imprecise terms. I may have complained about the uncertainty into which *Ough* v *King* plunged the 50/50 rule, when dealing with prescriptive rights, but that is a law of the Medes and the Persians compared with the flexible scale of the express grant. In another connection, I recently wrote about four ways of drafting a particular document (and there are no prizes for guessing that it was a party wall award), of which by far the worst was making one up for yourself. Of course, that is just what one usually gets in the documents we are now discussing: a form of words made up by a solicitor for himself – but sometimes amended by another, which may well make the situation worse.

I was recently asked to advise on a deed in which the clause granting a right of light to a certain Livery Hall was so widely drawn that, if you erected a flagstaff which could be seen by a man with his nose pressed hard up against the glass of one of the Hall windows, you would be offending against the grant. This was a disastrous predicament to have let oneself in for. I was also involved with another Livery Company which had succeeded, in the late nineteenth century, in binding their neighbours in fetters of iron, so that when the neighbours wanted to add a cubit to their stature (or perhaps a little bit more) the Company asked for a quarter of a million pounds. Measured in the usual way (to which we shall come in due course) the injury could not have been valued at as much as £50,000, but the wording of the clause was such that it was a question of: pay up, or don't build.

By contrast, some express grants do no more than give immediate rights to windows, as if they had acquired them by prescription – which follows later in this chapter.

So beware of express grants, and read them very carefully, before deciding how much protection they give you, or how much difficulty they are going to cause you in building. You know, if you have read other of my writings, how loth I am to involve the legal profession unnecessarily, but this is one time when I think it may be well worth while taking counsel's opinion, if the meaning is at all doubtful. Counsel may well echo a certain QC whom I attended in conference not so long ago, in saying, 'I do not say that there is not a great deal of money to be made out of arguing this point', but he will at least give an opinion, and your client will have more than your unsupported word to go on.

Implied grants are much easier to deal with. They only give rise to the equivalent of prescriptive rights (we're getting towards them, I promise) and they arise in virtually only one set of circumstances. When someone sells off a building with windows in it which rely on light passing over land retained by the vendor, that building gets an implied grant of light to those windows. It would obviously be a derogation from grant, and the purchaser would not get what he had bargained for if, as soon as he had bought his house/office/factory, the vendor erected a solid wall in front of the only important windows.

If you are the vendor and you want to be able to build in front of windows you are selling, you have to put an express reservation in the contract, and I dare say I shall have more to say about that later, particularly in relation to Newcastle-under-Lyme Squash Club. Note that any specific grant, express or implied, is almost certain to give rise to an immediate right. Other methods of acquisition take longer.

The lost modern grant is often regarded as a difficult concept to grasp. Many people (well, I at least) wish that it, together with time immemorial (to which we're coming) had been abolished when the Prescription Act (to which we are also coming, although you may be beginning to doubt it) was passed. However, it still exists and I have known it pleaded, though to little effect as it happened, in one case. The idea is that if you are enjoying a right over someone else's property, and they cannot prove that it is by permission which they can withdraw, then obviously you must have a grant somewhere entitling you to that right. The only trouble is, you can't put your hand on it just at the moment. Nevertheless, the fact that you must have had one at some time is so obvious that it is deemed to exist.

Let me make it clear: this is entirely a fictitious legal assumption. Everyone knows there wasn't a grant, and that you haven't just mislaid it. In one important leading case, *Dalton* v *Angus*, 1881, it was agreed on all sides that no grant in fact existed, yet it was presumed to do so for the purposes of the case. The most important point about the lost grant is that it may allow you several years in which to bring an action, whereas prescription (to which, etc.,) only allows one year. That is certainly the reason for its use in the case which I mentioned. The other use is in claiming against the Crown. You cannot acquire an easement of light against the Crown under Section 3 of the Prescription Act, 1832, but you can do so by other means. Since 'the Crown' covers quite a number of things as well as Buckingham Palace this can be quite useful: Crown Courts are one obvious example, and I had a couple of cases with the Post Office when that was a Crown body – and it used to deliver letters promptly and reliably as well, though my younger readers may find that hard to believe. The term of enjoyment needed in order to acquire a right under the lost modern grant is not laid down anywhere. It must certainly be longer than under the Prescription Act and obviously shorter than time immemorial (next paragraph), so I would guess at about thirty years' minimum.

I have never had a time immemorial case, and I would dearly like one to complete my set, so I repeat here the plea I made in an article in *The Law Society Gazette*, that if anyone is acting for the Jew's House in Lincoln (or similar) and needs my assistance, I should be pleased to give it – no doubt special terms could be arranged. Let me explain about time immemorial. If you can show that you have enjoyed a right since 'the time whereof the memory of man runneth not to the contrary', then that, too, like all these other methods of acquisition, establishes your right. Unfortunately, according to the law, that time is 1189, so it's a bit hard to prove.

Nowhere have I seen an official explanation of why 1189 is the date of legal memory, so here is my conjecture. Once upon a time (which proves it's conjectural, if not pure fiction) the date of legal memory used to be changed regularly. Every time a new king came to the throne (or perhaps on some other important occasion) the lawyers sat down and said something like: there's no man living now who can remember the Norman Conquest, so that's the date where we'll fix time immemorial. Then they fixed another date, and so on and so on until they came to 1189, which they probably fixed in 1275 or thereabouts. But another important event, or coronation, came along very soon afterwards, and they didn't bother to change the date; and next time they forgot; and next time it was so well-established that they didn't like to change it. So there it remains to this day. That's my theory, but if anyone knows the truth I'd be interested – though perhaps disappointed – to learn it.

And finally, at last, comes the Prescription Act, 1832. It was realised that the time immemorial method and the lost modern grant were a bit unwieldy, so the long title of the Act announced that it was 'an Act for shortening the Time of Prescription in certain cases', but unfortunately not, as I have already said, for abolishing other methods. Section 3 dealt specifically with rights of light, and differed in several important respects from the other sections. A comparative study is not necessary for our purposes here, but it needs to be remarked that, by not mentioning the Crown, it does not bind any Royal (or quasi-Royal) hereditaments. The period of prescription is set at 20 years 'next before some suit or action'. This means some legal action, not just 'doing something'.

The 20 years' enjoyment must be 'without interruption', and interruption is stated in Section 4 to require a period of one year. As you cannot have a year's interruption within a 20-year period after 19 years and one day have passed, it follows that effectively a right is acquired after the shorter period. You cannot, however, mount a legal action to uphold your right until the full 20 years is up: more of that later.

As is usual in these matters, there are allowances for disabilities, so that if you were a child, or a lunatic, or dead, for part of the time involved, that part has to be excluded. This applies not to the person claiming, but to the person resisting the claim to acquisition. As far as I know, it is no bar to your establishing an easement to have been dead for the first 10 years of the prescriptive period.

Finally, in this chapter, a word about the Rights of Light Act,

1959. This did not really have much to do with Rights of Light, but apart from its more important innovations, which are dealt with in a later chapter, it had an ephemeral effect which has occasionally given rise to some confusion. Because it was extremely difficult during the war years to stop anyone acquiring a right to light – perhaps I should explain to anyone to whom that period qualifies as 'history', that I mean the Second World War, 1939–45 – the period of prescription was extended for a limited time to 27 years. This relaxation has already lapsed, but I have known people to think that it was a permanent alteration and still effective. It isn't: we're back to 20 years' prescription.

To summarise this chapter, then. Of the ways of acquiring a right to light there abideth principally these five: express grant, implied grant, lost modern grant, time immemorial, and the Prescription Act; but the greatest of these is the Prescription Act.

Chapter 3

How to hold on to it

'It' is the right to light which you have so painstakingly acquired in the last chapter, of course. By far the best way of preserving light to your windows is to own all the land around, at least for a time, and then only to sell it off with a very clearly-expressed reservation, preserving as extensive a right as you wish. This counsel of near perfection is hardly available to any of us except the great estate owners, however, and so we shall have to consider other methods.

Eternal vigilance (and prompt action when needed) is essential, since only one year's interruption is enough to defeat a prescriptive claim – but the interruption has to be with notice, and acquiesced in by the dominant owner. The subject of notice is rather tricky, and I can't point to a case in which it was expressly discussed, but it would seem that it is not enough surreptitiously to obscure some light, and then claim that your neighbour has suffered interruption. I do not think, however, that you have to write to him and tell him.

Acquiescence, on the other hand, has acquired a useful leading case since the first edition of this book. In *Dance* v *Triplow*, 1992, the Court of Appeal decided that two and a half years' silence from either solicitor or claimant, even when objections had previously been voiced, would lead a reasonable man to assume that his neighbour had now accepted the situation. The Court distinguished the case from that of *Davies* v *Du Paver*, 1953, where the writ was issued thirteen months after the last previous objection. Since one has to acquiesce for a year, that acquiescence in the latter case would have had to begin only a month after a forceful protest – which was unlikely. In fact, between two large property owners this technicality is not likely to be insisted upon, if serious negotiations have been taking place, since next week/month/year the boot may be on the other foot. There is no doubt, however, that there are a number of bully boys around in the development world who would quite happily stand on the letter of the law if the little man next door should miss a trick, so do not allow too much time to pass before you issue your writ, if negotiations have stalled.

If you are sure that your light is injured – usually, after taking advice from a specialist consultant – you must get a legal action under way within one year of the injury occurring. The preliminary steps do not cost a great deal of money; they should ensure that your adversary knows that you mean business; and, provided that the advice you receive is sound, you should recover costs in due course.

It might be appropriate at this point to say a word about rights of light consultants. At the time of writing good ones are very thin on the ground. There are rather more people around claiming to be experts than I would rank in that category, and it can be rather expensive to rely on bad advice. Unfortunately, even the RICS does not test for competence those who claim to offer expertise in this field, and you would be well advised to ask more than one source for a personal recommendation, and go to the consultant whom most of them suggest. I'm afraid I won't be able to help all of you, however.

And now a word to those of you who may fancy yourselves as rights of light consultants, or are thinking of setting up your plate. In his book entitled *The Right to Light*, (Estates Gazette) my late father Bryan Anstey wrote, and personally inscribed in my copy: 'I sincerely hope that study of this book will not lead anyone to think himself an expert'. I would add that study of this work, too, will not make you an expert, although I have every intention that you should know very much more about the subject by the time you have finished reading it.

The difficulty is that not only do you have to remember all the law and all the little quirky decisions, some of which I hope to remember to tell you about in the ensuing chapters, but also you have to be able to make an assessment of the facts of the situation – whether there will be a loss and if so how great – and then put those two or three things together to advise on the best course to pursue. It is no coincidence that the three men whom I would rate as the top consultants all served very long apprenticeships to their predecessors.

Back to the main subject. It seems almost unnecessary to say so, except that a few cases have proved otherwise, but don't lightly enter into agreements with others which may give them the right to injure your light at a later date. Sometimes you may be seeking a concession from them: perhaps you are adding to your building in such a way that you are affecting their light and so, as well as paying compensation, you are being asked to enter into a deed which allows your opponents to rebuild in the future without so much as a by-your-leave. Your present proposals may put you in such a position that they could enjoin you if they so chose (and their chances of doing so are dealt with later) so that you either have to agree with their proposed deed or else alter your building. You may prefer to give in – but if you don't have to, don't.

As a kind of early warning system, be alert to planning proposals. If you can persuade the planners to refuse permission for a proposed building which would injure your light, it comes much cheaper than waiting until the servient owner has got permission and then bringing an action at law. As a matter of tactics, however, don't stress your intention to sue – if necessary – when talking or writing to the planners.

That might just, if they were hesitating, persuade them to grant permission, telling themselves that you will, in any event, be protected from ill effects, if any, by your legal rights. Keep more to the unneighbourliness of your opponents' proposals, by all means stressing the effect upon your daylight, but also bringing in matters with which planners are concerned though the law is not, such as sunshine, view, and general ambience.

It has taken at least 20 years for you to acquire your right to light. Don't throw it away by being slack in its defence.

Chapter 4

How to defeat acquisition

There are basically two ways to defeat acquisition, the theoretical and the physical, and the exciting thing about one of the theoretical ways is that it is theoretically physical. That remark is intended to intrigue you, and to keep up the suspense, I shall not deal with that aspect until the end of the chapter. As the chapters are all fairly short, at least you know that the suspense won't be intolerable.

Perhaps I should say, although it is so obvious that I had already started to write what will now be the next paragraph and have had to cross it out, that one way of stopping someone from acquiring any right is not to grant it to them. Do not, unless it is absolutely forced upon you in circumstances which make it impossible for you to refuse, concede a right to any windows which already exist or are being opened.

Any easement must (I have now written those words for the second time) be acquired *nec vi, nec clam, nec precario*: not by force, nor secretly, nor precariously. I know that it looks a rather silly literal translation, but I can think of no single other word which catches the flavour of *precario*. In fact it comes from *preces*, Latin for prayers, and came to mean 'upon request', or 'dependent upon the will of others', before it reached the definition we understand. It certainly means that you mustn't be likely to lose the easement at a moment's notice. The first two prohibitions are not really likely to apply to rights of light: they are more important in rights of way or *profits à prendre*. If you knock a man down every time he tries to tell you that you have no right to walk across his back garden to get to the bus stop, you cannot claim that you have always done so by right, and if you only sneak into the next door market-garden to help yourself to cauliflowers under cover of darkness, you can hardly assert your right to continue doing so in the daylight.

Precario often applies to windows, however. Deed after deed records that 'the windows coloured blue on the elevation lettered X-Y on the land coloured pink adjoining the land coloured green and hatched black on the plan lettered B enjoy their light over the aforesaid land coloured green by permission of the adjoining owners', or words to that effect. Whenever new windows appear, overlooking your land, you should therefore endeavour to persuade the owners of them to enter into some such deed or licence.

If you can so carry your point, you may be asked to limit your freedom to build for the future. You may feel able to agree to such a restriction, in which case you should try to be sure, firstly, that you stipulate a projected building which is big enough for anything you may want to do and, secondly, that the limiting clause is a permissive one, not restrictive. This is such a complicated issue that it demands a – short – chapter of its own.

It is not, in my opinion, necessary to have a formal legal deed in order to prove that windows have no right to light, although large corporations may well want to have one. A letter from your next-door neighbour acknowledging that he has no right to light would be quite sufficient, and you may well be able to extract one from him by threatening more physical measures if he does not comply – and I do not mean offering to knock him down, but see below.

If disposing of a property with windows, or land on which such a property may be built, while retaining other land (or even thinking of acquiring other land) over which such windows look or may look, do not forget to put a reservation in the deed of sale which allows you to build or to permit building regardless of its effect upon the light of these windows – or any other which may appear in that vicinity. You may never need the right, but it's silly to miss the opportunity of securing it, and it may well make your retained property more saleable should you later come to dispose of it as well.

So much for most of the theoretical ways. The physical ways are obvious. Block 'em up. I am tempted to leave it there, but perhaps I should expand a little. The best way of stopping any window acquiring a right to light is by stopping it from getting any light. No light, no right. If you are in a position, therefore, to construct a building before any windows looking at it have acquired any rights, stand not upon the order of your building, but build at once, and don't dilly-dally on the way to their acquisition. A really solid brick wall is definitely the preferable solution, but I suspect that a dense screen of evergreen foliage might be effective (and see the chapter on trees). You can also erect a fence, or put up a hoarding, and you can even construct curious devices to block one, new, window only, in a wall full of rightful apertures.

Near Hammersmith Broadway there is a metal screen about five feet square, looking for all the world like the back board of a basket-ball net (what a silly game it is, incidentally, with scores like 98–96: why don't they make scoring more difficult?) which was obviously put there to obstruct the light to a particular opening.

The difficulty about these physical obstructions, apart from the plant life, is that they may well require planning permission – which brings me to the theoretically physical. Before Town and Country Planning became all the rage after the War, the accepted way of stopping a window from acquiring a right was to erect a hoarding in front of it. Indeed, the thirteenth edition of *Gale*, published in the very year in which these matters changed, says: 'The conventional method of interrupting the access of light, in order to prevent the acquisition of an easement, is by the erection of a screen or hoarding near the boundary of the prospectively servient property'. That's what I've just said, only put more learnedly, and it means putting up some opaque object near the edge of your land, confronting the new windows. Unfortunately, since it became impossible to put up a fence more than 6 feet 6 inches high without planning permission, and since very few fences of that height would be any use in interrupting light (though, as a matter of fact one would have obliterated Mr Metaxides' light, referred to in the chapter on trees) it seemed as if dominant owners were going to find it a lot easier in future to attain their dominance. A way had to be found to redress the balance and, in 1959, as the second and still very effective part of the Rights of Light Act, a device was brought into being which put the servient owner back into much the same position that he had previously occupied. The only difference was that, instead of paying a builder to erect a hoarding, he now had to pay a surveyor, perhaps (good), and a lawyer (perhaps not so good).

What was this magical device? It is best known as a 'Notional Obstruction' – although I have found people dealing with such matters who did not know it by that title: let us hope that they buy this book. It is simply a paper substitute for a physical obstruction.

The procedure is as follows: if windows are about to acquire a right against you, you prepare a plan showing the windows and your boundary, and you nominate the size of notional screen you intend to erect (theoretically) along this boundary, which can be of unlimited height. You prepare a Notice of Notional Obstruction and you take it, with the plan, to the Lands Tribunal. They give directions on how it is to be publicised to the affected, would-be dominant owners, and when those directions have been followed, the Notice is entered on the local Registry of Land Charges, where it stays for a year. Thus, since one year's interruption is sufficient to defeat a prescriptive right, no such right is obtained by any immature windows, and they must start to prescribe all over again. If you are scared stiff that the windows are just on the point of attaining their majority, you can ask for immediate registration as a matter of urgency. The Lands Tribunal will, if satisfied as to the necessity, grant registration for four months, which will then be extended to the full twelve when proof of the subsequent publicity to the affected properties is produced. If you do not comply with the directions – and if, perchance, the dominant owner proves that he has already established his right – then the registration will lapse after four months and no interruption will have taken place.

It is, in the vast majority of cases, foolish to specify an obstruction of anything but unlimited height. In one of my very earliest cases, in which the other side seemed to be intent on playing games, they disclosed at the very last minute the fact that they were relying on a registered notice; they were actually careless enough to disclose also a letter from client to solicitor which said 'That should have them running round in circles for a bit' – or words to that effect. He who laughs last, however, laughs longest, and the precisely specified screen which they had registered did not in fact operate to deprive the relevant windows of light, so that to avoid a mandatory injunction – since they had gone on building in the face of our opposition – they had to buy my clients off at a very considerable price. There may be occasions when you are trying to obstruct some new windows in a wall containing well-established lights. That is the only time when you may have to specify some curiously shaped and detailed screen – or, indeed, you may be unable to do anything about them at all.

I propose to conclude this chapter with two problems which arise from notional obstructions, to neither of which do I have a really satisfactory answer, but I will put them before you as best I can. At least you will have been warned of their existence.

There is a theoretical answer to the first problem; I am not entirely happy that it always works in practice. When a notice has been on the local register for a year, it has done its work, and the notionally obstructed windows may then begin to prescribe again. If, however, someone searches the register, a short while later, what do they find? If they find nothing, they may conclude that the windows have a right to light. They should find evidence that a notice has been registered and that, therefore, until 19 years have passed since its year of registration ended, no rights will be established. I am sure that a search during the notice's actual currency will reveal its presence, but I have known a number of instances where searches during the following years have not shown up its former but still effective existence. If you have any reason to suspect that a notice may at some time have been registered – or perhaps even if you haven't – you should specifically enquire of the council whether one was on the register at any time in the preceding 19 years.

The second problem is a technical legal one, and no doubt a lawyer or two will write to tell me the answer. I can only tell you that I know of no case in which the issue has been tested. A notice of notional obstruction will defeat a prescriptive right, because one year's interruption is enacted so to do in the 1832 Act: but what effect will it have on an express or a lost modern grant? Consider. If you claim a right under the Prescription Act, one year's interruption defeats it. Therefore, you have only one year in which to bring an action to defend the right. The same is true of the effect of a notice of notional obstruction. You have the year of its registration in which to bring an action, after which the right is lost. On the other hand, if you claim a right under an express grant, or a lost modern grant, one year's interruption is not enough to defeat it. Therefore, you have several years in which to bring an action to defend the right. The same cannot be true, surely, of the effect of a notice of notional obstruction, particularly as that effect will cease when the year of its registration comes to an end. In that case, the failure of the 1832 Act to abolish other forms of prescription, coupled with the 1959 Act's intended simplification of obstruction, will have resulted in another little anomaly.

I think that one must conclude that registration of a notice under the Rights of Light Act is only effective against windows which have not yet acquired a right: it would not work to deprive windows of rights which already existed. Ah well, it's stuff like that which makes the subject so fascinating.

Chapter 5

How to deal with someone else's right

There are really only two ways to deal with other people's rights of light: build and chance it; or ask them how much they want. A very little-used way is, of course, not to injure their light at all, by keeping within the envelope of the previous building but, as I say, this approach does not find much favour.

I achieved a certain notoriety from one such case, however. There were a number of really tricky situations arising out of a proposed redevelopment so, working together, the architects and I had trimmed the building to the state where, at all sensitive points, it was wholly within the existing profile. A great meeting of the professional team was summoned by the clients, and we all assembled in a massive hall: there must have been 50 of us, including clients, architects, quantity surveyors, engineers, services engineers, Old Uncle Tom Cobley and me. Tea and biscuits were served, and the proceedings began. Each element in turn was asked to report on the state of the game from his point of view, which each did, at some length. When my turn came I stood up and said (and I give you here my entire speech): 'Everything we propose to do is either covered by deeds or, being within the existing building's outline, has no effect on the neighbours'. And I sat down again. 'Isn't there anything else you'd like to say, Mr Anstey?' asked the head client. 'Yes', I replied. 'I've been trying to get another biscuit for ten minutes'. They didn't ask me to any more meetings.

There is no duty at law to go and negotiate with anyone who may have a right to light: you are not committing a criminal act by building even in such a way as drastically to reduce the light to their most important windows. You are, however, taking an awful risk.

The risk is that your building works might be injuncted. (Technically, the word is 'enjoined', and I am not one who believes that because language is constantly changing, all changes are to be welcomed. I despise the incorrect use of 'hopefully' or 'parameters', and the lack of distinction between 'imply' and 'infer', while very few people seem to be able to discriminate between 'effect' and 'affect'. However, I approve and find helpful the use of injunct as a root word and, as long as one sticks to injunctable and not injunctionable, I think that forms deriving from it can be used without shame.) I go into much more detail about injunctions and their possible cost to the dominant owner in the chapter on remedies, and I utter there a warning about overstepping the line between damages and an injunction which I am also going to put forward here, but in this chapter I am really looking at things from a developer's point of view, be he a multi-million-pound property company or the householder building a bedroom over the garage.

An injunction is a disaster. True, you may recover damages yourself if the application for an interlocutory one was ill-founded (see again the chapter on remedies), but you're bound to be out of pocket anyway, not to mention the nuisance and disturbance of it all. However, let us assume that the adjoining dominant owner was not so silly as to rush off to court without being advised that he had a good case, and that the injunction is not only sought but obtained. What does the developer do then? He probably looks around for someone to blame and, if possible, sue, and the architect is likely to be the principal candidate. If he had a rights of light consultant who had advised him that he was free from risk of an injunction, then the consultant might as well flee the country.

An injunction stops you dead in your tracks. The wording of it will be to the effect that you cannot build so as to injure the light of your neighbour, and that probably means that you will be confined to the outline of the previous building on your site. Your foundations may be all wrong for such a building, and the planning of your accommodation may be completely disrupted because you can no longer put the core where you intended. Your programme will run late, you may have to renegotiate a letting, you'll be out of pocket on costs and you won't have the amount of space to let that you thought you would have. As I said two paragraphs ago: a disaster.

I explain at length in the chapter on remedies how to tell whether your building is likely to be injunctable or not, but if your new structure is substantially larger than the old, and there are some important windows very close to it, then it is highly likely that you are at risk. You have either to build and chance it, which in this case might be unwise, or to reach an accommodation with your neighbour. The only other possibility is to trim your building so that its impact upon next door is less severe.

If you decide to approach your neighbour, the matter has to be handled with great delicacy. It's not really the best tactic to say, 'I'm going to ruin your light, and you could get an injunction to stop me, so how much does it need to buy you off?' That is rather asking to be taken advantage of. It's equally unwise to assume brashly that you can get away with it, and try to pooh-pooh the other side's rights. That is likely to put their backs up instead, with much the same end result. The best approach is an open and friendly one, but with a degree of confidence. 'You know that I'm about to build next door. Here are my plans. I think that your light may be injured a little, and of course I'm perfectly ready to pay the proper sum in compensation. If you would like to instruct a consultant to agree the money with mine, I'd be pleased to pay his fees.' There's no guarantee that the dominant owners – or their consultant – may not reply 'I'll see you in court' or words to that effect, but at least you have given yourself a chance.

Many people think that a sign bearing the words 'Ancient Lights' has some secret and wonderful powers, and that unless you have such a sign, your windows will never acquire their right to light in its full potency. The sign means nothing, and has virtually no value at all, except that it proclaims to the world that you think you have a right to light, and are likely to be strong in its defence. If you see such a sign on someone's windows which you are going to affect, you should watch out. You should almost certainly make a direct approach, because you would not look convincing if you tried to tell the court that you didn't realise that your neighbour had any right to light.

Surprisingly often, you may be able (or able to advise your client) to build and chance it. Adjoining Owners frequently don't notice that they have been injured, and all the money which they might have claimed is saved. In taking such a course of action, however, you have to be sure of two things. Firstly, that you or your client realise what the awful consequences of a succesful application for an injunction would be when the work was well under way; and secondly, that there is very, very little chance of such a thing happening. If you're advising a client, and you fail to warn him of the risks, a writ served on you is likely to follow hard upon the heels of the writ on your client. I think, though, that there are times when you can and should advise your client that he can and should take the risk, as long as he appreciates what the risk entails.

Paradoxically, there are lots of times when Adjoining Owners who can't tell Stork from butter – or a view from daylight – will shout and scream, and even issue writs, when their right to light has clearly not been actionably injured. Those persons just have to be shown the error of their ways, and persuaded to shut up and go away.

Finally, in this chapter, a word about clients who demand that you should have all the rights of light tied up before the contractor starts on site. You can, of course, tell him to find another consultant – a course which seems to recommend itself to me more and more frequently – or you can explain gently to him that the only way of doing that is with a series of blank cheques, and with a large number of co-operative opponents. The pace of discussions is dictated by the injured party, the dominant owner, and if he doesn't want to rush, the only thing that is likely to change his mind is a really substantial offer, well over the odds, with a time limit attached for his acceptance of the bribe.

If you want to buy someone out of their rights (which, the courts have stated time and time again, you must not think you are entitled to do if they are unwilling) you have got to go about it in a conciliatory way, and at their speed. Any urging them along must be done delicately and politely if you do not wish either to bring the negotiations to an abrupt halt or else to put up the costs to your client by a large 'impatience' factor.

Chapter 6

Permissive and restrictive deeds

There is a great deal of confusion as to what constitutes a restrictive deed and what is a permissive one. There are some documents which partake of both natures, and some which are so open-ended that you wonder why anyone ever bothered to pay solicitors to draw them up. This last kind can be a snare and a delusion to poor innocents, who fancy that they must have some tremendous impact upon future development on one or the other – or both – sides and yet they are no more important than a 'release', a very simple document employed in straightforward cases by rights of light consultants, to conclude matters without the need of legal assistance.

A typical release runs thus:

Address Head Office............
or House of...........
the dominant owner

FORM OF RELEASE
RIGHTS OF LIGHT
Re: The Injured Building and the Proposed One

In consideration of the sum of (so many pounds) the receipt of which is hereby acknowledged, and the payment of fees in the sum of (rather less money) direct to (the dominant owner's surveyors) we consent to the erection by (the developers) of a building substantially in accordance with the attached drawings nos. (124–125) and undertake for ourselves and on behalf of anyone claiming interest through or under us to raise no objection to such building on account of any interference with light.

For and on behalf of
The dominant owner
Signed The Boss...........
Date Whenever...........

The other day a client called me in for urgent consultation about a rights of light deed. When I read it, it said in effect no more than the above, had no bearing on any current or future matters, and yet had probably cost a great deal more to prepare, and beyond doubt taken a great deal longer to have executed than the simple form illustrated. Then it had been carefully preserved by the parties, to waste my time and their money with considering it.

The most important kind of deed, which does need careful keeping and consideration, is the restrictive kind. This says something like: 'The building owner may build according to the attached plans, but no variation from those in any building or rebuilding is to be permitted without the consent of the adjoining owner'. Actually, to tell the truth, it probably says nothing like that at all, because it is all tricked out with legal phraseology, but that is what it means to say, when all superfluity is stripped away. However it is worded, you must carefully scan each deed to see if that is the meaning that lurks within, because to ignore such a prohibition is to court disaster.

The virtually certain remedy (see that chapter) for breach of a specific prohibition on building is an injunction. Clients of mine went to counsel once about a deed which permitted them to build up to 50 feet high all along a certain frontage. They proposed to build 40 feet high for ninety per cent of the length, and 55 feet high for the remainder. The net result would be that the owner with the benefit of the agreement would be better off than if the full freedom of the clause were adopted, yet counsel advised that they were at serious risk if they built those extra five feet without seeking their neighbour's consent.

Escaping from a prohibitive deed can be very costly, even if relaxation is sought before ever work starts. If the other side discover the deed after you've started work, then they have you over a barrel indeed. I heard of a case recently where over two million pounds was paid for release from the constraints of such a deed. I have no hesitation therefore in repeating myself: examine all deeds minutely, and look very carefully for any such restricting words. You must find them if they exist, and explain their import fully to your clients.

Permissive deeds are more complicated. If that seems paradoxical, it is because while it is usually fairly easy to understand what is prohibited, it can be very difficult to understand what is permitted or indeed whether the permission is wholehearted or modified. Very often the permission granted to the side which was not building when the deed was drawn up can be very simple. As part of the price extracted for allowing the first developers to build at all, the erstwhile dominant owner has insisted upon a clause allowing him in future to build anything for which he can get planning permission. On one or two remarkable occasions, wily lawyers have even succeeded in persuading the dominant owners to allow the developers that freedom, while restricting their own ability to build in the future. I have wondered what the dominant owners' own lawyers were thinking of to let them sign such a document, but not every consideration which goes into an agreement appears on the face of the document.

It has nothing to do with deeds, but that last remark reminds me of one of the last cases which my father handed over to me on his deathbed. He had hung on to it so long, he said, because he smelled something fishy in it. He was right, too. I was acting for three dominant owners against a developer who was advised by very skilful lawyers, as well as a consultant who was negotiating with me. I forget the exact figures, but let us say that I was claiming ten, twenty, and thirty thousand pounds for my three clients, and the other consultant was offering eight, fifteen, and twenty-five thousand. Imagine my astonishment when the first client contacted me to say that he had settled for five thousand. I at once wrote to the other two and told them to watch out. Surprise, surprise: shortly afterwards the second client settled for ten thousand. I impressed upon the third clients, who were well known to me, how careful they should be, but to no avail. I soon learnt that they had sold out for twenty thousand pounds. Note that, in each case, the settlement figure had been less than was already on the table from the other side's consultant. What was the explanation? To this day I have not found out, but when I read deeds granting inexplicable favours to one side or the other I remember this case.

The real problems come with what I can characterise as the 'but no other' class of deed. Many documents contain a clause which permits a development up to certain dimensions, but no further; or it may allow a building in accordance with the attached plans, but no other. It is far from clear whether the plain and ordinary meaning of those short clauses is prohibitive or permissive. When they are interlarded with legal verbiage it becomes even harder to be sure which meaning should attach to them. It is hard enough even to explain the ambiguity, but I will try.

The first view of the meaning of many such clauses is that their effect is: only the nominated building is permitted; any other building or any variation is prohibited. The second view is that it means: the extent of the permission granted by this deed is stated above, and it doesn't extend any further; if you go beyond these limits you will be subject to the ordinary constraints of rights of light law.

The trouble is, of course, that as I have already complained, people (by which I mean solicitors) will insist on writing their own versions of these clauses, instead of following a really reliable model, which I would be perfectly happy to provide for them. You have to read each such clause word by word to try to be sure of knowing which kind you have got.

Although I have told the story elsewhere, I must retell here the history of the potentially most expensive clause of this kind which has come my way. I think that it would be no exaggeration to say that millions of pounds rode upon the precise interpretation. A deed was sent to me by solicitors, together with counsel's opinion that it was a restrictive one. I read both deed and opinion carefully, and responded that, with all due respect to counsel, whom I knew well to be of high repute in the field, I thought it permissive. My 'opinion' was sent to counsel, who replied that, with all due respect to me, he adhered to his original view. As so much hung upon the issue, my clients went to an eminent QC to decide the matter. His opening words have since become one of my favourite quotations: 'I do not say that there is not a great deal of money to be made out of arguing this point'. He went on to say that if he was forced to side with one or the other, he would reluctantly disagree with his learned friend and agree with Mr Anstey.

At this point, the real, arrogant, conceited and juvenile Mr Anstey would have liked to be dancing around counsel's chambers with his hands clasped above his head like a triumphant boxer, waving to the crowd. It appeared to those present, however, that Mr Anstey sat modestly hearing this decision, his features revealing no hint of satisfaction or triumph. Perhaps as he sat there he remembered the occasions on which he had been just as thumpingly wrong.

Another kind of ambiguity is sometimes found in deeds which attempt to reserve certain rights to vendors or lessors: and I am not just speaking of an isolated example. More than once I have met clauses which begin by reserving the right for the grantor to build anything he wants on his retained land, regardless of its effect upon the light and air of the land disposed of, and end by saying that he can do so provided he doesn't injure the light and air of the buildings on that land. Don't ask me what such clauses mean. I haven't the faintest idea. A lady is supposed to have asked the poet Browning what a certain poem meant, and he replied: 'Madam, when I wrote that poem, only God and Robert Browning understood it. Now only God does'. I suspect that much the same is true of those who cobbled together such contradictory deeds.

There are two morals to this chapter. The first is to read all deeds with the utmost care to see into which category they fall. The second is to try to ensure that any deeds into which you have any input should be expressed with unambiguous clarity.

Stop press. I have just received a legal opinion on at least one set of 'but no other' deeds. Counsel's view was that they were not restrictive.

Chapter 7

Trees (and the like)

The position of trees in the rights of light world is far from clear. In the case of *Metaxides* v *Adamson*, 1971, it was held that to grow a screen of greenery right outside a window which had just been allowed to be opened was derogation from grant, but the planting followed hard upon the opening. No-one that I know of has yet been taken to court because of the slow and natural growth of plants, and I am far from sure in my own mind that the courts would treat deciduous and evergreen trees identically.

I have been involved in a number of cases involving trees, but only one of them (the aforementioned *Metaxides*) actually went to court, and my role in that case was limited to taking photographs for my father, and then making coffee for him and Keith McDonald while they sat in my living room discussing the case. Many years later, I was invited to lecture to the annual conference of the Arboricultural Association, and I offered the members – a fruitful source of such cases, one would have thought – that I would take any such case at half my usual extortionate fees, provided that it went to judgment. As it has not produced any takers yet, I repeat that offer here.

All I can do in this chapter is to tell you about some of my undecided cases, and how they might have turned out. Perhaps the most interesting involved a new town. One of the residential areas had been carved out of a wood, and within that wood stood a very ancient cottage. Some trees were included in the gardens of the new houses and, after a while, the owner of the cottage sued the owner of one house on the grounds that, since he had owned the house, the trees in the garden had grown to such an extent that they injured the cottage's light. My evidence was going to be that the effect, if any, of the alleged growth was small, and an arboricultural colleague was going to attest that, over the centuries, particular trees might grow and die, but the general height and density of the wood was likely to remain much the same. The suit was dropped: wisely, in my opinion, since I am sure that the defendants would have been successful.

In another case, my client was offended by the growth of a thick evergreen hedge outside her kitchen window. There was no doubt that her light was being affected and, if I remember correctly, the hedge had been deliberately planted by the neighbour. (Not deliberately to spoil the light, you understand, but for aesthetic or gardening reasons.) This matter was solved when the neighbour was persuaded to trim – and promise to keep trimmed – the hedge to a reasonable height. I think that my client might have won that one.

Another example I can give is of a case when I was consulted to avoid the prospect of legal proceedings. A client sought to ensure privacy for himself in his garden by planting a screen of trees around the perimeter, but he was anxious not to plant any where they might offend the neighbours. I was therefore shown the planting design, and asked to comment. I took the view that if any tree immediately affected the light of any windows to a marked extent, it would be susceptible to an action, and that if its growth in the first few years after planting caused any losses, there must be a risk there also. I therefore changed the sizes of a few trees and moved a few, and have heard no more, so I think that I probably got it about right.

Rumour has reached me of a case where an injunction was awarded against some trees or plants, but I have none of the legal details. I really would be grateful for any solid cases of which my readers could inform me, and my half-price offer above is genuine and seriously intended.

On a slightly different tack, but still on trees, beware of tree preservation orders (TPOs). Even your own trees can affect your light, of course, and you may be prohibited from pruning them.

I had a client (whose son had been at school with me) who had some limes at the pavement side of her front garden, which was a mere 20 feet or so in length. Every year for 30 or 40 years these limes had been pollarded so that there was adequate light in the winter to the front room. When a TPO was made on all the trees in the street, my client raised no objection – indeed, she was all in favour. However, when she had the limes pollarded as usual, the council threatened her with imprisonment, or a substantial fine at the very least. I was asked, and was able, to give evidence that the living room would have been plunged into Stygian gloom if the limes had been allowed to grow unchecked. I believe that a satisfactory accommodation was arrived at.

On another occasion, I was asked to provide evidence about the darkening effect of a tree upon a room whose light had already been affected on the other side by the activities of a previous client of mine. The solicitor against whom I had formerly acted rang me up in some distress because his wife had been threatened with condign punishment for having the tree felled in their back garden. I was relating this case to the Arboricultural Association, and told them that my client had only had the tree cut down on the spur of the moment when, according to my story, an Irishman came to the door and asked if she wanted any trees felling. (I knew it was an itinerant, and picked an Irishman because I could do the accent.) To my astonishment, a man in the audience got up and said: 'He wasn't an Irishman, he was Yugoslavian. I know, because I was the Council Officer in charge of the case'. That will teach me to embroider my anecdotes. I believe that there was a happy outcome to this story too, and that my clients were let off with a caution – certainly, they have been back to me for other advice since.

Since I can offer you no really solid advice on where you stand with trees and light, I must just advise you to approach any such coincidence with caution. On the matter of cutting down trees, however, I can be more forthright. Don't: unless you are absolutely sure that they aren't protected in some way.

Chapter 8

Abandonment

No-one knows what constitutes abandonment, that is to say, giving up a right which you have acquired, not even your omniscient author. It is a matter of the facts in each case, or what the judge had for breakfast. That remark is not quite as light-hearted as it may seem, nor is it intended as a jibe at judges. There are a number of matters about which my opinion fluctuates according to whether there is an 'r' in the month: for example, about God and creation. Half the time I think that the world is so complicated that only God could have created it; the other half I think it is so complicated that not even God could have devised it. What I will try to do here is to give you a few guidelines on what definitely does and what definitely does not count as abandonment.

A mere temporary failure to use light certainly does not lose the right. There is a leading case in which shoe boxes were piled against the windows, and believe it or not, I have had at least two such cases myself, where the other side have argued that my clients, the shoe company, were not entitled to the light because they themselves had piled boxes up to obstruct it. I also advised on another case, from the opposite side, where it was television packing cases which blocked the light. I was confident in advising that the contents, actual or erstwhile, of the cases made no difference to the application of the law. To legal eyes, the boxes are transparent.

There are two very interesting examples of case law on abandonment, one presuming it, the other rebutting it. In the first, a chap pulled down his wall which had windows in it, and rebuilt it imperforate. When another chap came along and put up a building near the wall, the first chap starting putting windows back in again, and brought an action against the later builder for obstruction. He lost.

In the other case, a church was pulled down and the site was going to be sold, so some poor innocent put up a building next to the vacant site. Much to my surprise – and to his, no doubt – the

Broken reveals, with the brick infill bonded into the wall, indicate that there is probably no intention ever to use the window again

Church Commissioners succeeded in their action against him. I would be very interested to know how much, if any, injury the servient building caused, because it is my experience not only that churches are very hard to injure, but also that when novel points of law are decided, the facts of the actual injury are very often barely considered.

Most often, the question which the practitioner will have to consider will relate to bricked up windows. It seems, from the leading cases, that the courts will want to be convinced of the dominant owner's clear intention to abandon his right. The test I always use to decide on the intention of the window owner is the state of the brick reveals. If the joints have been broken in the

Straight reveals, and a brick infilling panel, indicate that there may be an intention to reopen the window at some future date

closing, then I am convinced that the window has been abandoned; if there are straight joints, then it is possible that it may be intended to take down the brickwork and reopen the window at some future date. I may still be prepared to presume an abandoned window in some circumstances where there are straight joints, but never the reverse where the joints are broken.

In the case of *Marine and General* v *St. James' Real Estate*, 1991, the judge held that, precisely because the reveals were unbroken, the windows had not been abandoned. As it happens, the changes inside were so radical that I might have made this one of my exceptions.

A puzzling case with which I once had to deal had a very gratifying ending. A client was proposing a development alongside a building – I've a feeling that it was an ice-cream factory – which had a number of lofty windows facing towards the site. They were going to be so badly affected that I recommended a direct approach to the dominant owner. 'But the windows have been abandoned', protested the architect. 'They're completely blocked by breeze-block walls inside'. I replied that I thought that they did not count as abandoned, and that the walls had probably been put there while the site was a prey to vandals. 'Mark my words', I said, 'When your building goes up, the breeze blocks will come down'. Several years later I was relating this case, while talking about abandonment, to a Society of Architects in the same borough as the development. I told them that I did not know whether my words had come true, but a man stood up in the audience, and said 'You obviously don't remember me' – this was certainly true, but then I once failed to recognise a millionaire with whom I had lunched only a fortnight before – 'but I was the architect on that job. The walls came down, and the windows are now being used'.

Time comes into the equation as well. This is particularly true when we are talking about abandoning a right, rather than abandoning an actual window. Whereas interruption for a year (physical or by the theoretical device of the notional obstruction) is sufficient to defeat a claim under the Prescription Act, an action under a lost grant or time immemorial will lie for rather longer. At one time I was of the opinion that such an action would be subject to the normal limitation of six years, but two distinguished firms of solicitors have strongly argued that it is not a question of a single cause of action, and that therefore the limitation period does not apply. They say that a breach of one's easement is a continuing nuisance so that the question as to whether one has abandoned one's right or not is a matter of fact and degree for the court every time. I'm not wholly convinced, but I do understand what they're saying. However, if you continue their argument to its logical extent, it must follow that every injury to light that has ever been suffered must remain actionable until the windows are abandoned, and that must be absurd. I still tend to think that the courts would show extreme reluctance to entertain a claim for a loss of light which first occurred more than six years ago.

So you see, it is a matter of using your own judgment in most cases, relying on a mass of experience and having read really helpful guide-books, full of useful examples.

Chapter 9
Alterations

Shakespeare said: 'Love is not love, which alters when it alteration finds', and to a great extent the same is true of light and the right to it. Your right to light is to receive light through a defined aperture; it is not just a general right to all the light and air that may happen to be floating about over the next-door field, or whatever. It is my opinion that the law has gone rather further than it might have done in accommodating changes in windows.

Most of the leading cases are confusing largely because, I suspect, the courts don't really understand the science of light. This becomes evident if you study their remarks about 'pencils of light' and 'cones of light', neither of which concepts (if either can be dignified by that word) is much help in the exact measurement of sky visibility through partly-overlapping windows.

In one leading case, *Tapling* v *Jones*, 1865, it was much argued whether Mr Tapling, having substituted new lights for old, had made himself liable to obstruction by Mr Jones, even when he reopened the old windows. It was eventually decided that he had not abandoned (see that chapter) his old windows unequivocally, and that mere alteration did not lose their right.

Obviously, if you enlarge a window you are not making things more difficult for the servient owner. If he succeeds in obstructing your new big window, he would certainly have injured your little old one. If you make your windows smaller, then you are imposing an additional burden on the chap next door and, although the case law is not clear on this point, I think you would not succeed in an action unless you could prove that the old larger windows would have been injured just as much as the new smaller ones.

When you are dealing with the same sized windows, but just shifting them about a bit, I think that one can rely on the words of Farwell J. in *News of the World Ltd* v *Allen Fairhead & Sons Ltd*, 1931. I'm not sure whether it was his father or some other relation whose judgment in *Higgins* v *Betts*, 1905, he quoted so approvingly, but he then tried to apply the test of nuisance laid down by that worthy in a case where there was very little coincidence of windows. (This is where the pencils come in.) His important paragraph began with the words used by all judges when there has been a lot of argument about the law, and they are about to reject one perfectly reasonable side of it. 'The true view is this'. (In other words, 'I think'.) Unless the injury to the small coincident bit of window is in itself enough to amount to an actionable injury, the dominant owner cannot restrain the servient owner from building.

An amusing incident arose in one case about whether moving the plane of the windows affected the right. The judge was just about to decide that a wall 5 feet 8 inches back from its former position was not the same wall, when someone pointed out to him that he hadn't got to make any decision on the windows in that wall anyway. This, therefore, cannot rank as a decision, not even as *obiter* or *passim* – perhaps 'might have been' is as high as one can put it.

A more helpful case is one in which a wall had swung through a slight angle, so that the change in its position varied from 1 foot to 3 feet 5 inches. It was in the Court of Appeal on this matter that the misleading cones of light were referred to, but at any rate they and the court below concurred in holding that the right had not been abandoned by moving the wall. It seems, therefore, that you are safe in moving the plane of your windows by a foot, probably all right if you move them an average of 2 feet 3 inches, getting a bit dubious if they shift 3 feet 5 inches, and almost certainly out of court if it's 5 feet 8 inches.

A general rule, which I have propounded elsewhere, is to remember congruent triangles. If all the angles and all the sides are equal, triangles are congruent. It's the same with windows: the closer everything is to how it was before, in size, shape, position, plane, and even as to numbers and relation to the other parts of the building and other windows, the easier it is going to be to prove identity of burden. No congruity, no continuity of right. In order to prove the identity, it will be a very good idea to have kept a reliable record, both photographic and surveyed, of the former apertures.

The question of internal alterations is a bit more tricky. I think, but I am not sure that the law supports me, that one is only entitled to light to areas which have been lit for the prescriptive period. You can't suddenly enlarge your room and thus increase the burden on the servient owner so that when he builds, one year later, an extension which would not have actionably injured the light to your room in its earlier state, you can now claim against him. There is a case in which a judge argued that if he enlarged his dining room, that was up to him, but I don't think that the point about converting an innocent building into an offending one was argued before him: he was simply considering how far the injury extended. Even there, however, I would be against him.

Although the use to which a man has chosen to put his light neither increases nor diminishes his right – so that whether he is temporarily using the boardroom as a cleaner's cupboard or vice versa is irrelevant – I am sure that if he physically alters the layout of his premises it can substantially affect the position of the servient owner.

Let us take two simple examples. The old room was twelve feet deep from the window, by ten feet wide, all well lit. A building is erected opposite which would limit the adequate lighting to seven feet deep into the room. In the original state of that room, no actionable injury would be suffered. Suppose that just prior to the building opposite being erected, the dominant owner knocks down the back wall of his room and makes it twenty feet deep. The same

If the partition is taken away, I think that, for 20 years to come, only the effect on the front area has to be considered if a new building is erected opposite

effect on the lighting by the same building would now produce an actionably injured room. It cannot be right that, without prescribing for it, the servient owner can suddenly make life much more difficult for the dominant owner.

In the second example, the case is reversed. A twenty foot deep room is partitioned (more or less permanently) so that it is now only twelve feet deep. Can the dominant owner now claim that the servient owner's building has injured his prescriptive light? I would say not, because I would argue that he has abandoned the right to light to the larger room, by building the partition.

If a permanent partition is inserted, I think that the dominant owner has abandoned any right to light behind the new wall, although at least two eminent gentlemen disagree with me

I repeat that I do not find the law altogether clear on these points, but have given my understanding of the position. Quite a few cases involving some of these subtle alterations of the dominant tenement would be likely to end with the judge giving his 'true view'.

Chapter 10
Remedies

The basic right of anyone who has established a right to light is to retain the light to a minimum standard. Originally, there were no two ways about it. If your light was injured you got an injunction restraining the development, or having it pulled down; and if you couldn't prove an injury, you lost your action and the building continued.

In my book on *Party Walls and what to do with them*, I mentioned with approval certain ancient writings, and they are just as relevant and interesting on the subject of rights of light. Vitruvius, who wrote around the year dot, plus or minus fifty years, gives a very good basic rule for establishing whether an injury has been suffered, concentrating correctly on whether there has been a loss of sky visibility. A ninth-century Byzantine emperor, Theophilus, is recorded as hearing a rights of light claim against his wife's brother, Petronas, whose palace extension was blocking out an old lady's light. Her right was upheld and Petronas was publicly flogged. I dare say that some dominant owners would like to see such a penalty brought back into use. A book published by the London Record Society, part-edited by my former history tutor Dr Helena Chew, deals with the London Assize of Nuisance, 1301–1401, and gives details of several rights of light cases. For example, in 1341 Geoffrey Aleyn complained that the parson of St. Stephen's, Walbrook, had obscured windows for which there was a right to light. He satisfied the mayor and the sheriffs as to his right, and the defendants were ordered to remove the impediment within 40 days. By contrast, in 1343 Rose de Farndon complained that Hugh de Brandon was building so as to obscure the light which she had enjoyed across a street called Goderom Lane for 'time out of mind'. Hugh proved that the land had always been built on, and so Rose lost her action.

Matters went on being decided in a similar way for many years, by which time many people had come to think that there were some cases in which an injunction was altogether too dramatic a remedy

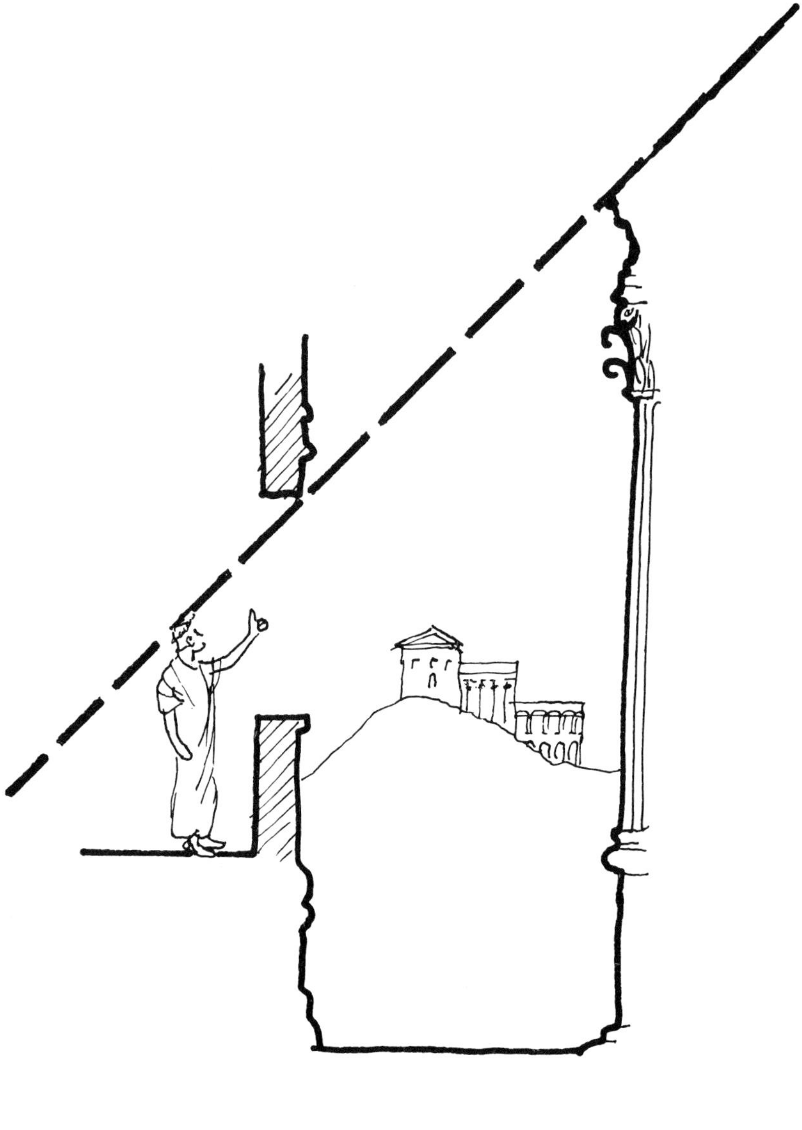

Vitruvius had a good idea of how to assess a rights of light injury, and gives this Corinthian building the thumbs up

to deal with small injuries, at least in the courts of equity. In common law it had been possible to obtain damages, but plaintiffs didn't always know or choose the correct channel for their actions, and could be referred from one court to another. The Chancery Amendment Act of 1858, usually known as Lord Cairns' Act, gave the Court of Chancery the power to award damages in lieu of an injunction, if it seemed equitable to them so to do. (It has now been superseded by Section 50 of the Supreme Court Act, 1981).

The way in which the courts should address themselves to the question of an injunction or damages was much clarified by *Shelfer* v *City of London Electric Lighting Co*, 1895, in which four tests were laid down to be applied. They were, and are:

1. is the injury small?
2. is it one which can be estimated in money?
3. would a small money payment be an adequate remedy? *and*
4. would it be oppressive to the defendant to grant an injunction?

Two of these questions are easy to answer, one difficult, and one impossible. Let's deal with the easy ones first. It is fairly easy to estimate most losses of light in money terms. I have admitted elsewhere (*The Valuation of Rights of Light*, Calus, 1981) that I might have difficulty measuring the value of an effect upon a notable stained glass window in a cathedral (I have a case involving such a window in a church currently before me), but I would reckon to be able to cope with most domestic and commercial cases – and even some ecclesiastical ones. You will be given some advice on how to do so in the chapter on valuation. It is usually straightforward to decide whether the defendant would be harshly treated by an injunction. If he has acted openly, and the plaintiff has watched his progress without a word of complaint, and then seized the most damaging time to bring an action for an injunction in the hope of being bought off with a considerable bribe, then the plaintiff is not likely to win the sympathy of the courts. If, on the other hand, the defendant has tried to keep the plaintiff as much in the dark as he can, while the plaintiff has protested at the earliest possible moment, an injunction is far more likely to be awarded.

Now we come to the difficult one: is a small money payment an adequate remedy? The question is easier with commercial properties than domestic ones, but not entirely straightforward with either. If you own a building worth fifty million pounds and your light is so seriously affected that the damage is valued at one million (and I have never yet met so extreme a case) then you are in exactly the same position before as after. Before, you have £50m worth of building; afterwards, you have £49m worth of building and £1m in cash. But what about the occupier of the building? Even if you have not reserved the rights to yourself, the money may not compensate him in the same way. You can afford to take the broad view, but can he? The answer may turn on the impossible question, to which we will come in due course.

In a house or flat, the answer may depend upon what room or rooms are affected. Roughly in order of lighting importance, I would say that the rooms of a house are: living room, kitchen, dining room, bedroom, bathroom. If you live in a house grand enough to have more elaborate rooms such as a ballroom or a library, you can afford to consult me personally as to where those rooms rank. If the injury is a serious one to either of the first two rooms, I am certain that test number 3 has been failed, and if it is to either of the last two I think that it might well be passed. To the middle one, I would say that it could be more seriously injured than a living room and still pass, but couldn't take as severe a blow as a bedroom. A family room/breakfast room is half and half living room and kitchen, and behaves accordingly.

It is impossible to know what is meant by small. I haven't read any cases in which the matter has been specifically considered. My father once asked an assembly of very learned lawyers what 'small' meant and, according to him, they went into a sort of huddle from which the oldest and wisest emerged, stroking his long white beard (still according to my father's version) and said gravely: 'Well I should say' – dramatic pause – 'that it would not be large'. A lot of help, I must say.

Let us return to our £50m office block. If the light to one room, 12 feet square, is obliterated, that can only be a small injury to the building as a whole. But if that room is the only office of a small firm, it will be a dramatically large loss. What if the word small applied to any one room? Does the loss have to be small, or the injury (because, remember, you can sometimes lose a lot of light before suffering an injury at all), or does it depend on how much light you had to start with? If you only had a little light, a very small loss can represent a serious change for the worse. In that connection, my father was very fond of the image of the noose. If a man has a noose around his neck which dangles to his waist, you can take in a lot of slack without doing him any harm; but if it is already tight around his neck, one twitch may be enough to send him to eternity.

'Small' must be a matter of judgment, knowing all the circumstances. If you get any good decisions, write and tell me.

It must be emphasised that all four tests have to be passed, not just one or even the majority. Furthermore, their general tenor must always be borne in mind: if the injury is not trivial, damages are not a sufficient remedy and an injunction will lie. This was always the ruling in *Shelfer*, and Lindley L.J. said in that case that 'the court has always protested against the notion that it ought to allow a wrong to continue simply because the wrongdoer is able and willing to pay for the injury which he may inflict'. A few years later, in *Cowper* v *Laidler*, 1903, Buckley J. said: 'The court has affirmed over and over again that the jurisdiction to give damages . . . is not so to be used as in fact to enable the defendant . . . to purchase from the plaintiff against his will the legal right to the easement'.

Over the years that followed, however, it seemed to me that the see-saw had gradually tilted in favour of the defendant, and the tests were being applied in a way that said, in effect: 'Is the injury serious? If not, the remedy is damages'. By 1984, in other words, the exact opposite of the original question was being applied, and I wrote articles and papers saying that this was what was happening. Then came *Pugh* v *Howells*, and the Court of Appeal reaffirmed, in the strongest terms, the words of A.L. Smith L.J. in *Shelfer*, when he emphasised how reluctant the courts should be to allow the servient owner to buy himself out of his breach of the dominant owner's rights.

Anyone who seriously injures his neighbour's light must, in the context of these cases, put himself at grave risk of an injunction. The courts will be particularly inclined to penalise him if he has carried on in the face of vigorous protests from his neighbour, or even if it can be shown that his own advisers had counselled caution – as had happened in Pugh's case. The intending developer should therefore think very carefully about the potential cost of being stopped in his tracks by an adjoining owner. He would do well to consider, at this stage, whether or not to modify his proposed building or extension before next door – or the courts – get to hear about it. It may be that, if his architect can produce a satisfactory solution with a smaller profile, it will pay to show the larger solution to the opposition first, and allow them to 'force' the developer to cut back his scheme to the already prepared position, which may well make both sides happy – always a desirable result.

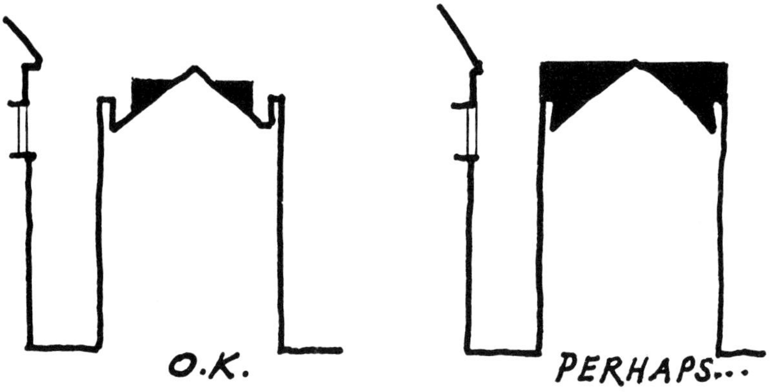

You could certainly build the extension shown in the first picture, and probably the one shown in the second

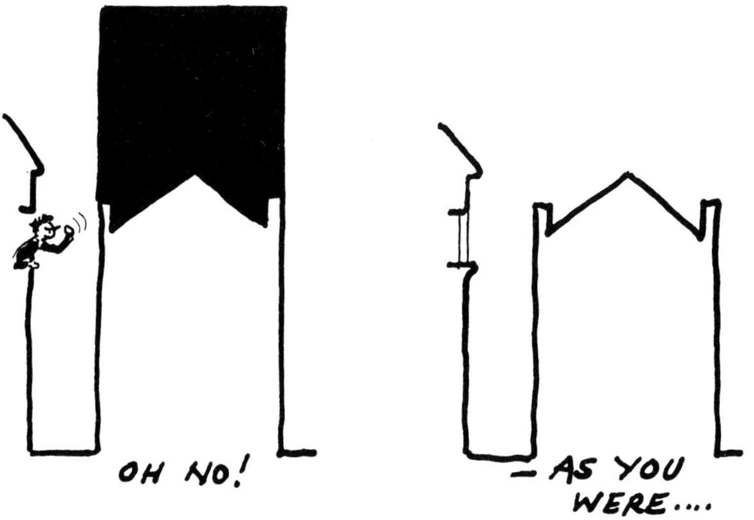

If you tried to get away with the third, and your irate neighbour obtained an injunction, you would not be allowed to build either the first or the second, but constrained to stay (or return to) where you started

The reason that so much care must be taken in avoiding provoking an injunction is that it will, in all probability, restrict the would-be developer to an obstruction no greater than the former buildings on the site: it will not allow him to commit a moderate injury. Since he can be fairly sure of getting away with damages for a small injury, he should consider whether it is really worth going for a much larger building which might be stopped altogether.

The risks are not all on one side, however. If the dominant owner wishes to bring an action to restrain a development, having been unable to negotiate a reasonable settlement with the developer, he must consider how he is going to go about it. He will certainly express his action as being for an injunction and/or damages, but the real question he must decide is whether to go for interlocutory proceedings, or to let the action take its normal course. If he chooses the latter, building is very likely to continue pending the trial of the action, and counsel for the defendants will doubtless make great play with the fact that he did not go for interlocutory relief. Despite all that I have quoted above, it is very unlikely in such circumstances that the courts will issue a mandatory order for the pulling down of a completed building, and the plaintiff will have to be content with money.

The threat of an injunction is, of course, a potent one, even if it is lying there waiting for a full trial of the matter. In a notorious recent case, *Blue Town* v *Higgs and Hill*, 1990, the defendants applied to have the action struck out unless the plaintiffs applied for interlocutory relief. The Court virtually acceded to this novel line of argument, but a case soon after, *Oxy Electric* v *Zainuddin*, 1990, cast grave doubt on the correctness of this decision, and did not follow it.

It may be that some of my readers are not familiar with interlocutory proceedings, and so I will explain why the plaintiff finds himself on the horns of a dilemma. If you think that your light is going to be really badly affected, and only stopping the building will save you, you can ask a judge, at very short notice, to stop the work immediately (or to halt publication, or whatever your particular action is about; this isn't just true of rights of light cases). He will do so if you can make out a *prima facie* case and, as is usually so in building matters, the balance between the parties can best be maintained by putting everything into suspense until the full case can be tried, perhaps some months later. But, and it is a very big but, he will only do so if, normally through counsel, you give 'the usual undertakings'.

Obviously, every plaintiff would like to stop the wicked developer in his tracks, but it is 'the usual undertakings' which deter him. If he loses his action, the plaintiff has undertaken to make good to the defendant all the costs which have been incurred through the cessation of the work – as well, of course, as the costs of the action. The building costs will include any extras charged by the contractor for taking his men off the site and bringing them back again, any increases in material or labour costs which have arisen during the delay, and possibly interest lost on the money laid out on the site while idle. Only two classes of people – apart from those who are absolutely downright sure they are going to win – can afford to give such undertakings: the very poor, and the very rich.

I assume that the courts would look very closely at the case presented by someone who had not the means to honour an undertaking, before granting interlocutory relief, but I am pretty sure, too, that they would not look favourably on counsel whose sole argument for resisting the proceedings was that the plaintiff was a small man without much financial backing. That does not mean that they would give an interlocutory injunction automatically to someone just because he could afford to pay if he was wrong.

At a conference with a very able rights of light (and other matters) senior counsel, I once asked whether the plaintiff would always be called upon to honour his cross-undertaking if he failed to win a final injunction, but was awarded damages. Counsel said that, obviously, if he got his injunction, there could be no question of the undertaking; if there was clearly no case to answer or if it had been a case where damages were always going to be sufficient remedy then, in all probability, he would have to pay up; in his opinion, however, if the courts decided on balance to award damages after weighing the possibility of an injunction, the plaintiff would not have to bear the developers' costs of the delay. A short while afterwards, I was at a social occasion with the aforementioned barrister and a junior (but experienced) counsel from the same chambers. I asked the latter whether he had any comment to make on this view of the situation, and he asked the senior counsel what authority he had for his proposition. Drawing himself up to his full height of about six inches less than his junior, he said: 'You have my authority'. Well, I have received no better statement of the position.

Chapter 11

How to measure light

I once received a letter from a young surveyor who claimed to have studied for several years under George Wakefield, and therefore to be probably the best-qualified person in the country to measure loss of light to a building, by taking light-meter readings at various points on the face nearest an obstruction, and in the rooms behind. I replied, with customary modesty, that I was generally reckoned to be the best person in the country at measuring the loss of light in buildings, and that while I was full of admiration for George Wakefield on the subject of photographic lighting, the use of meters in legal cases was singularly ineffective. The young man was subsequently persuaded to consult a real expert.

The reason that meters are useless should have been obvious to a person experienced in photography. The trainees in my office have just persuaded me to buy them an absolutely idiot-proof all-singing and all-dancing camera, because they claim to be incapable of such difficult technical feats as deciding whether they are taking a close-up or a distant view. I, however, prefer real cameras, such as Exaktas, Super Ikontas and, in a daring rush towards the modern, Nikon F2s, and almost always use a Weston Master meter. If you are taking photographs in England (for a magnificent book on *Abbeys*, for example) you take a separate meter reading for each shot, even if it is only a few minutes since you took the last one, because the light from an English sky changes all the time. You cannot, therefore, use a light-meter or photometer to measure the amount of light in a room before the offending construction begins, and then do the same again when it is complete, and hope to obtain comparable readings, because it is virtually impossible to be sure that you have exactly the same sky conditions to measure a 'before and after' set of daylighting circumstances. It is therefore essential to find a method of measurement which is not affected by fluctuations in the actual intensity of light received from the sky at any one moment.

The amount of the sky itself which is visible from a certain point only changes when obstruction, temporary or permanent, obscures it. Clouds or bright sunlight make no difference to the sky visibility, and it is therefore this factor on which the science of measurement and the law have chosen to concentrate. In fact, the brightness of the sky varies by about six to one between summer and winter, but the same patch of sky will always be there, until someone puts a building in front of it.

Sunny or cloudy, winter or summer, rain, hail or shine, the patch of sky visible through a window remains the same, even though its brightness may change – until someone shoves a building up there

In 1932, an International Conference on Illumination, meeting at Cambridge, calculated the amount of light available from the whole dome of sky. (If you were monarch of all you surveyed, from the centre all round to the sea – like Alexander Selkirk – you would see the whole dome of sky.) In the middle of an overcast day in winter it amounts to five hundred foot candles, that is the equivalent of five hundred standard candles one foot away from the object, or as we would say today, 500 lumens. I am told by Michael Cromar, always more up-to-date in these matters than I, that if I really want to be correct I should talk about lux – but you know me: imperial measurements, pounds, shillings and pence; and lumens is as far as I am prepared to go. They also decided that one lumen was adequate light to do work involving visual discrimination, and that light should be measured at the working plane. (I am only assuming that they made these last two decisions: they all work together for good and someone must have made the supplementary decisions which make the whole system work, so who more likely?)

It follows mathematically from the above that if one five-hundredth of the whole dome of sky can be seen from a point on the working plane, then at that point you have one lumen: enough light to read the small print of *The Independent.* I used to say *The Times*, but even my adherence to tradition has not glued me to that paper when a better one arose. One five-hundredth may also be expressed as 0.2%, and this is the way in which you will usually meet it. By drawing a line between a number of similar points you will obtain a 0.2% contour. Everywhere on the working plane between that line and the window will receive at least one lumen; everywhere behind it will receive less. You will always need to draw two contours. The first contour will be of the 0.2% sky factor as it is or was in the prescriptive conditions, before building activity started on the servient tenement, while the second contour will show the condition now that that construction has taken place, or what it is expected to be when the building is complete. By measuring the movement from one contour to the other you can estimate the effect of the change.

I explained in the chapter on 'What is a right to light' that, as a general rule, if 50% of the working plane in a room still received 0.2%, or adequacy, the light to that room is generally considered not to be actionably injured. In order to make this chapter complete in itself, I will repeat the explanation about the 50/50 rule here. The test I have just outlined was accepted for many years as being almost absolute: certainly practitioners treated it that way. If 50% was still well lit, there was no injury. In the case of *Ough* v *King*, 1967, the judge relied on a view and, not being trained to judge light, decided that a room just over 50% well lit (note that 'adequate', 'well lit', '0.2% sky factor', and 'one five hundredth of the whole dome of sky' all have very similar meanings) was nevertheless injured. I should point out that the reason I criticise this decision so severely is that I believe that the judge made his inspection at a time when any room would have seemed dark, and he was not capable, in my opinion, of imagining what the light would have been like at some other time, in some other season, or in some other circumstances. Furthermore, he was substituting uncertainty for certainty, and whereas before that case a consultant, if he had done his measurement accurately, could advise a client with confidence that a building had either been injured or not, nowadays no-one can be absolutely sure about anything.

In my opinion, the 50/50 rule is still a good working guide, and can safely be adopted for commercial cases. In domestic cases you can be sure that less than 50% adequacy is an injury, pretty sure that over 55% is not, and worry about it in between. That 'worry' is the big difficulty in residential jobs.

The test of an injury is not how much is taken, but how much remains: that is why there is so much emphasis on the dividing line between an adequately and an inadequately lit room. It is once you step over that line that things start to happen. That is why it is so irritating not to have a definite line to measure, but to have to utter words of warning, like 'If one accepts the 50/50 rule, but remembering *Ough* v *King* . . .'. After an injury is known to exist – to one party at least – then it is a question of whether the appropriate remedy is an injunction or damages. That is certainly a matter of fact and degree in each case, and one could not expect a hard and fast rule to be laid down on such a delicate subject, but I would like to see the courts set a fixed standard for injurious/non-injurious affection, so that consultants could give definite advice to clients, one way or the other.

Deciding whether an injury is injunctable is the most difficult task that the rights of light consultant has to undertake during the course of a job. Carrying out the Waldram diagram calculations (to which you will be introduced in a couple of pages' time) may be time consuming and is certainly not easy until you get the hang of it, but the value judgement on 'injunctability' is extremely tricky, and if you get it wrong you will possibly ruin your client – and perhaps yourself as well. This is certainly true if you are acting for the developer. Acting for the injured party is a lot easier. You can always tell the developer that you are going to seek an injunction, and thus leave his consultant to worry about your chances.

The chapter on *Remedies* goes into more detail about the likelihood of an injunction or damages, while that on *Valuation* explains how the different amounts of injury are assessed in money terms. In this chapter I am only concerned with actually measuring the effect in physical terms.

It is regrettably still necessary to say a word or two in discussing the so-called 45° rule. My father said, in his book, that he hoped that he had done enough to kill it off once and for all, but it seems not, and so I'll try yet again to dispose of this fallacy. That the 'rule' sometimes works can be likened to saying that all cats are black, and relying on the fact that quite a few are. Unfortunately, many architects are under the impression that if an obstruction falls below a line drawn at 45° to the sill of a window, the light of the room served by that window cannot be injured. This ignores

The 45° fallacy: 1
What lies behind a window is very relevant. The same obstruction will injure a boardroom, but be harmless to a cloakroom

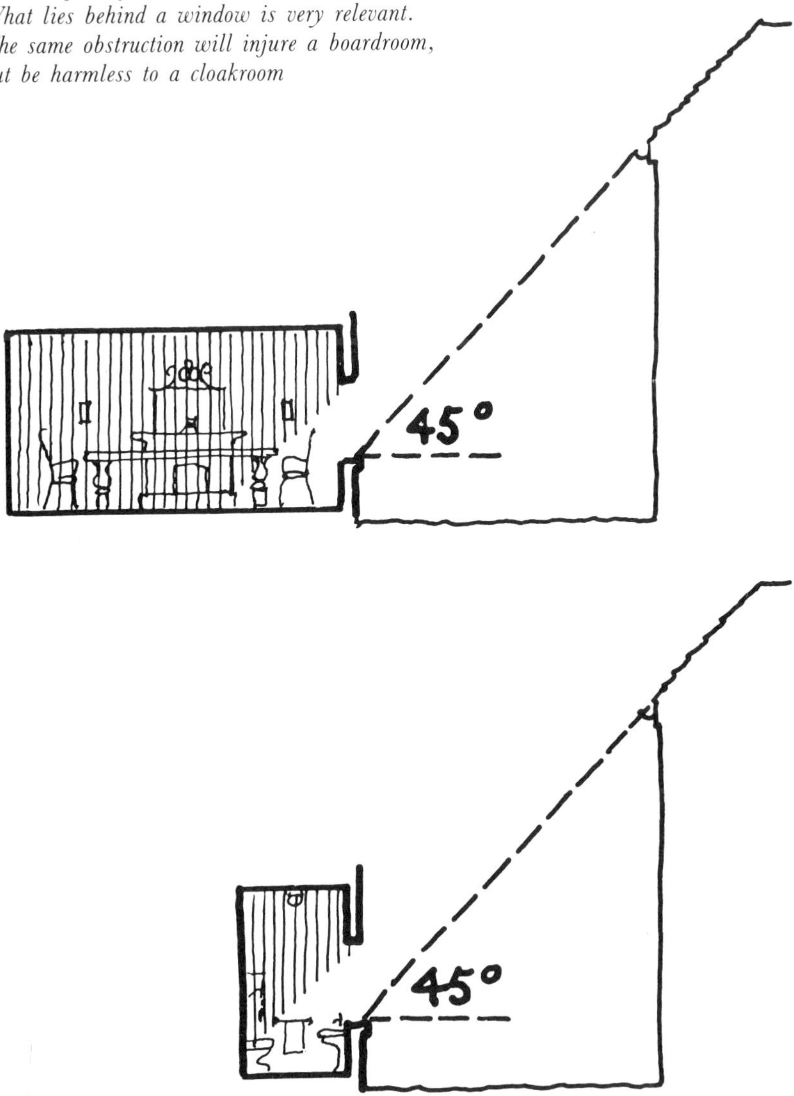

completely the layout of the room behind the window and a simple sectional elevation will soon make this clear.

It seems an awful waste to spend so much time in proving a negative, but I have met so many cases where people have gone astray in relying on this so-called rule that it may be worth one more try to teach them better.

The height of the window, too, can be very relevant, as another illustration will show.

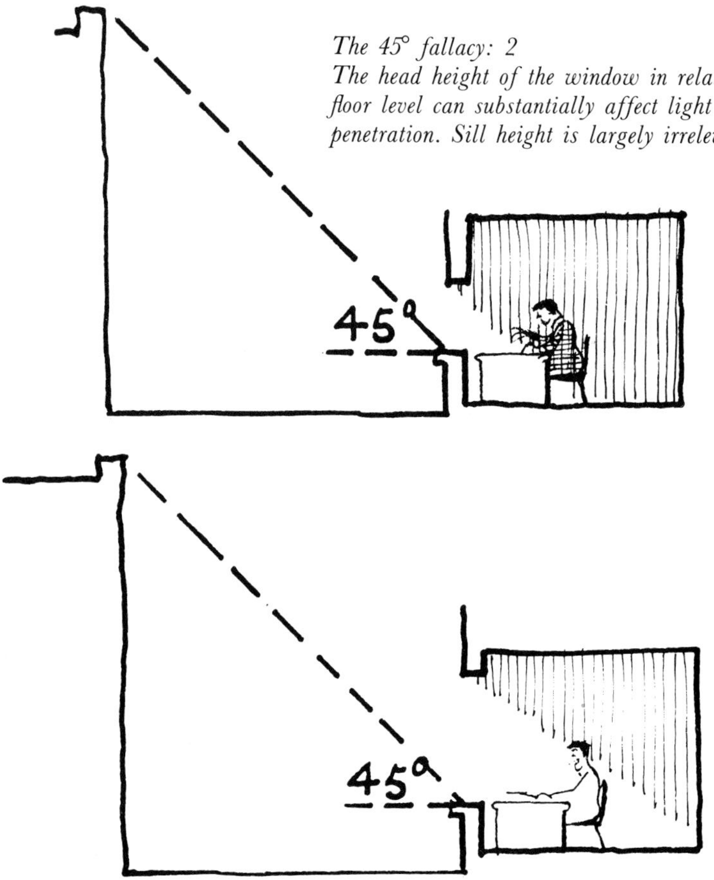

The 45° fallacy: 2
The head height of the window in relation to floor level can substantially affect light penetration. Sill height is largely irrelevant

It would be convenient if the tests shown above were all that was necessary, or those which are recommended by Vitruvius. A simple line from the building opposite to the head of the affected window is certainly a much better rough and ready guide than any line from the sill. However, it is by no means enough.

Far and away the best method of measuring sky visibility within a room is by using the Waldram diagram. This was 'invented' by

Percy J. Waldram and is a method of showing on a flat piece of paper, and from thence on to recognisable floor plans, the curved and three-dimensional effects of the real world. On to his diagram you plot in plan and elevation the outlines of the window you are studying, measured from a suitable point in the room at table (2 feet 9 inches: I am told that is 85 cm, but I shall ignore that information) height. The unglazed, or masonry, opening of the window is used for your calculations, because glazing bars and the like may change, while the basic aperture is likely to remain unaltered. Then from accurate surveys you plot the existing obstructions to light, not forgetting distant ones which may be relevant, and you produce a curious curved picture in which a patch or patches of sky will be found. These are measured, and can be compared to the whole dome of sky at the same scale – a single Waldram diagram shows half the whole dome (which is itself a hemisphere). If the area of the patches is greater than 0.2% of that whole dome, you pick a point further back in the room and try again. If it is less, then you move forward.

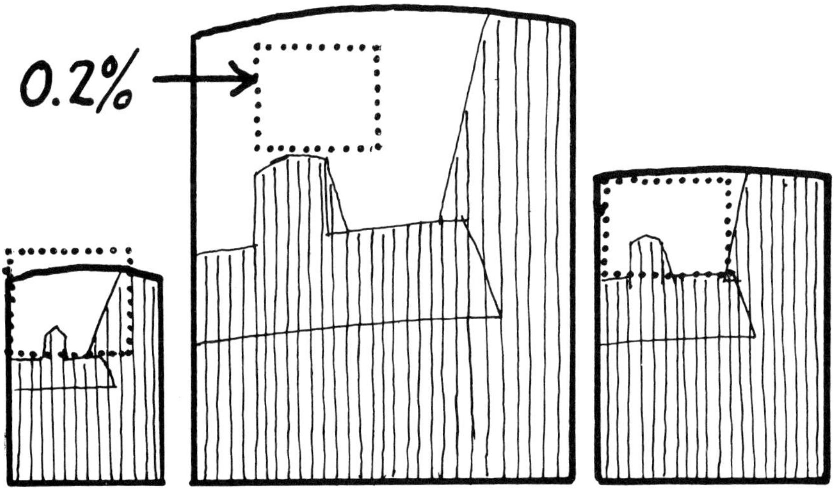

Not too little, not too much, but just right: the patches of sky which may be shown up on your Waldram diagram studies. If you obtained the first image from your chosen point, you should try another one, further forward; if the second, you should move backwards in the room; if the last, cheer, and move sideways

When you have plotted enough points, you can draw a contour of 0.2% sky visibility. The whole exercise is then repeated for the new conditions and a second contour drawn.

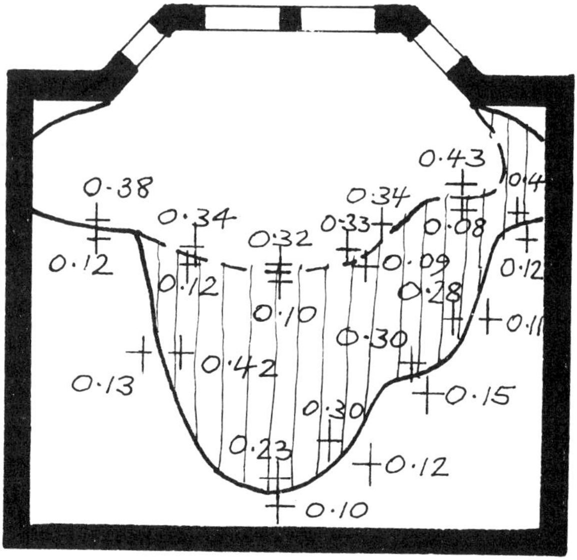

The solid line represents the 0.2% contour in the 'old' conditions; the dashed line shows the 'new'. If may be necessary to study many points within a room in order to obtain the two contours, but it is not necessary to find the exact 0.2% points on those lines. You can extrapolate from near misses

Sometimes the starting point for your 'before' contour will be an agreement. The building you are studying may be the subject of a deed which permits it to be carried up to a certain height, but in fact it is intended to make it higher still. In that case, your 'before' contour is not that which shows the light as it is at present in the dominant premises, but what that light would be if the permitted building were carried out.

You are now in a position to assess whether any injury has been/will be suffered/caused. I put these alternatives because you may be carrying out your assessment on behalf of a dominant owner or a servient one, and you may be doing so before the old building is taken down, after the new building has gone up or, the most difficult, when the old building has gone and the new has not yet come.

The experienced rights of light consultant learns to reconstruct, in his mind, buildings that have long – within the meaning of the Act – been demolished, using clues like the remnants of an old flashing, or brickwork which was obviously not intended to be exposed to the weather. The maps produced by Charles E Goad Limited are very useful in this respect. By finding an edition for the appropriate year you can often get a very good idea of what buildings were formerly on a now cleared site. Sometimes, indeed, all that needs to be done is to complete a terrace, mentally. The consultant has also to try to create in his mind a new building or a new extension – as high as that sill, and as far out as that tree, for example – or a complete new office block, with a three-storey podium and a ten-storey tower. You can realise that making an on-site estimate of the likely effect of that sort of building is both difficult and dangerous. You can only risk it when you're very experienced and the result is not likely to be critical.

If you are acting for the dominant owner, looking from inside the may-be-injured window, it is a lot easier to guess and, on the whole, less serious if you get it a little wrong. In the vast majority of cases, however, accurate surveys of the existing conditions, relating the site of the proposed building to the possibly affected windows, are absolutely essential, and must be very accurate indeed for any case which is going to court. The rest of your evidence is not likely to be regarded as reliable if cross-examination shows your plans to be inaccurate. When you are assessing the situation for a potential developer, however, you can hardly walk in next door and say: we may be going to affect you, so can we have some plans, please. There you have to rely on much less accurate measurements, and the client has to be told of the limitations. You will probably have to count brick courses and estimate distances, and even that without being observed to be doing so.

I remember one case where I had to lean out of a window and guess at an effect some hundred feet away or so and round a corner: I guessed at 'a couple of thousand pounds' damage. Later, I was able to get close, and said 'about ten thousand pounds'. When I was able to measure it from inside, because a claim had been made, it came to fifteen thousand pounds – the claim had been for forty. The client was not best pleased at this escalation, but I was able to point out that I had always expressed the inaccuracy of the method of assessment I was being forced to use. With hindsight, I wish I had expressed it even more forcefully.

You must be careful to take account of all relevant obstructions. A distant tower block may fill a very critical gap in the skyscape, while a large chimney stack in the old conditions may be enough almost completely to negate the effect of a new storey upon one window, while making no contribution to the effect upon another. Make sure that a photographic record, at least, of your client's old building is taken before it is demolished, while in critical cases nothing less than a full survey is desirable.

'Since crooked figure may in little place attest a million' the relationship of large chimney stacks on the 'old' building to the windows in the dominant tenement can be equivalent almost to an entire storey on the 'new' building

Photographs alone can be very misleading, and a few carefully noted measurements can save hours of poring over confusing photographs. Sometimes, of course, you will have been instructed too late, and will have to rely on what can be found: I remember one case in which three of us stared through magnifying glasses until we were dizzy at an old photograph in a newspaper office, trying desperately to work out what the old obstruction had been. If you are taking the photos, try to take them so that they relate to each other, and to an OS map on which you have marked the points from which they were taken. Note also whether they were taken from the roof, ground level, or where in between.

When considering a proposed building (and old ones too, for that matter) look out for the plant rooms. Architects don't think that they're very important, and they will often be missing from early editions of plans, to be added on at a later stage. They can be critical to rights of light, however, since they very often form the effective skyline to be considered.

You may not always be asked simply to measure 0.2% contours. In one case I acted for tenants whose landlords proposed to substitute tinted glass for clear in their windows. The tenants were concerned that this would mean a substantial reduction in daylight within their offices, and I was asked to calculate the effect. We obtained figures of translucence for the new material from the manufacturers, and then worked out what percentage sky factor would be needed to obtain the same amount of light as clear glass would produce from 0.2% of sky. The loss was then shown by the variation between those two contours.

If you do find yourself going to court try, with the approval of your clients and lawyers, to agree your plans with the opposition. If you have made a mistake, it's better to find it out in conversation with your opposite number than in open court, and if he has, it may be that you can persuade him that his side ought to withdraw, or at least change their tune.

A lot to do with rights of light is a matter of opinion, especially since *Ough* v *King*. The actual measurement of sky visibility, however, can be an exact science, so you should use your very best endeavours to see that you carry it out with the utmost precision of which you are capable and which the circumstances allow.

Chapter 12

Valuation

I have actually written a whole book on this subject. It is all of fourteen pages long and published by Calus, but the practice, if not the law, of valuation has changed a little since I wrote it in 1981, and therefore even those who have bought and read it are not excused from reading this chapter, especially as the very simple diagram shown in that book has led to some confusion as to areas of loss, which I shall attempt to explain a little more clearly in a couple of pages' time.

If you follow the principles which have been adopted by the leading practitioners, you should find little difficulty in the valuation of rights of light. If you argue with them, I contend that you will end up proving that in fact they work.

Let me first of all discuss a few methods which do not work. One is to ask the local estate agent how much he thinks the value of a property has diminished. He is not trained to consider the loss of light alone, and will usually take into account all sorts of extraneous matter – not to mention the fact that he may have a sad tendency to give the answer which he thinks the client wants to hear.

Another unreliable method is to attempt, even at a sophisticated level of valuation, to assess the effect upon a building as a whole. This can lead to lengthy argument based on unscientific premises. The whole building method is useful however, in dealing with those who argue that because of its prime position the building has not actually suffered any loss in value because of its loss of light: those who put forward this argument also like to say that their new building has increased values in the neighbourhood, and that for that reason no loss has occurred – quite the contrary in fact. Your building, or your clients' building, they argue, has actually had its value enhanced by their development: so why are you claiming? Ask such a person to imagine two absolutely identical buildings, both improved by their new neighbour, and both enjoying all the same benefits except one: the light of one is the new conditions, the light of the other is the old. Would your adversary bid the same by way of capital or rent for the two properties? If he says that he would, you might as well give up talking to him and see him in court. If he honestly replies that he would not, you explain that your valuation exercise is directed at finding out by how much his bid for one should exceed his bid for the other. The answer equals the loss suffered.

Now to the approved method. In the chapter on measurement you learnt how to draw contours of adequacy in old and new conditions. The area over which the contour moves is the area of loss.

Sometimes, owing to a great change in the shape of the servient building, there will be areas of gain as well: these must be deducted from the losses. The area of net loss must be very carefully calculated, using a planimeter or geometrical means. It can help to apply a grid of square feet to the area of loss.

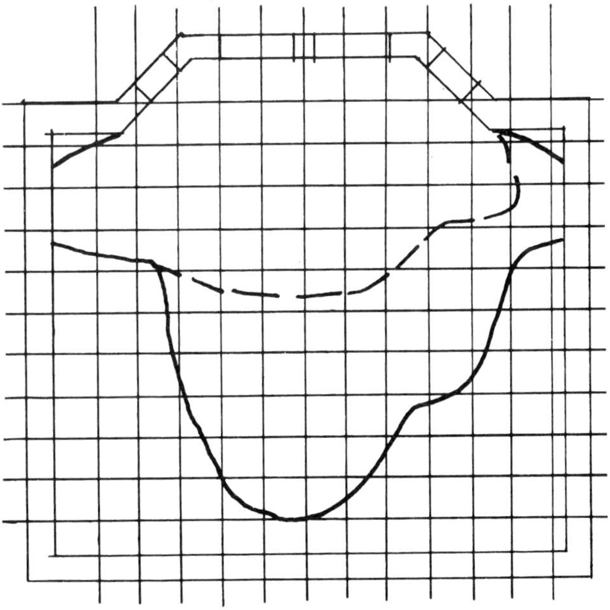

Applying a grid of square feet makes it comparatively simple to measure the loss of well lit space in the area between the old, solid line and the new, dashed one. I make it about 38 square feet on a quick look. Check it for yourself

The grid will make it easier for you to check all the necessary measurements: room area and 50% area, together with well lit areas lost and remaining.

It is also necessary to measure the area of the whole room in order to be able to assess firstly, whether there has been an injury, and secondly, if there has, how serious it is. You will remember that I recommended sticking to the 50/50 rule for most normal purposes: your next task is therefore to measure how much of the room remains within the 0.2% (well lit) contour. That must then be expressed as a percentage of the whole room area, so that you can decide whether to proceed any further with the valuation. I will repeat that, in commercial cases, if the area still adequately lit is over 50% you may fairly safely say that there is no injury. If you are dealing with a domestic case, you will be in some doubt between 50% and 55%, but fairly confident at over the latter figure.

When you have a whole set of measurements – I'm telling you all this in the order that I do it, but unfortunately, the reason for doing it doesn't appear till a little further on, so for the moment you must just follow me blindly and learn the purpose later – of the room, the area remaining well lit, and the area of loss, you must produce a table from them which, in my office, looks something like the one on the opposite page.

You will now see the reason for all the measurements which you have so painstakingly calculated, counted or guessed. The half room area is a fundamental calculation, together with the area remaining well lit, because if the latter is greater than the former there is no injury in that room, at least if you adopt the 50/50 rule. Don't forget, however, that if one room is actionably injured, other rooms in the same ownership can also come into the loss calculations, even if they would not rank as actionably injured on their own. The second floor rooms in the table opposite are two such. They come under the heading of parasitical injuries, about which I shall say a little more near the end of this chapter.

In the next few paragraphs, I shall examine another example, where the maths may be easier to follow than in the table of real-life figures.

The front, first, second and makeweight areas are all part of the net loss area, and the efz stands for equivalent first zone, which is a reduction of the other areas by arithmetical means. The system works like this: let us assume a room area of 200 square feet, an old well lit area of 160 square feet, and a new of 30 square feet. One way of expressing that loss would be to say that it was 130 square feet, but in the method adopted by the leading consultants, the area of 130 square feet is broken down into very serious loss, serious loss, fairly important loss, and not very important loss, which correspond to the four headings mentioned at the beginning of this paragraph.

Rights of Light:

Table of Areas (nearest sq. ft.) & Analysis of Loss

FLOOR/ROOM	WHOLE ROOM	HALF ROOM	PREV. +0·2%	NEW +0·2%	LOSS	Front	1st	2nd	Mkwt	EFZ
6/1	716	358	698	85	613	68	179	366		464
6/2	108	54	107	10	97	17	27	53		79
1/1	88	44	69	39	30		5	25		18
1/2	188	94	96	60	36		34	2		35
1/3	389	194	267	111	156		83	73		120
2/1	107	53	107	70	37				37	9
2/2	24	12	24	20	4				4	1
				Totals:	973	85	328	519	41	726

A table of atypically large losses, as produced in my office for working out equivalent first zone areas, from which compensation is eventually calculated

We consider that any loss which falls into the area of the room between 50% and 25% well lit is standard, or first zone loss. In the example I am examining, that would be exactly 50 square feet. Any loss between 50% and the rest of the room would not be actionable in itself, but does form part of the loss once an actionable injury has been suffered by the loss creeping over the 50% line – more than creeping in this example. That injury is therefore reckoned at half value, and a shorthand way of doing the calculation to which we shall eventually come is by halving the area. The 60 square feet of loss is therefore shown in the second zone column, and eventually equals 30. Similarly, in the table 366 square feet in room G/1 gets added in as 183.

If any loss is serious enough to impinge on the first (or last, depending upon how you look at it) 25% of the room, its importance means that it needs to be multiplied by one and a half, producing, in this case, 30 instead of 20 square feet, and 68 for G/1 equals 102. It is when the front zone figures start to mount up, by the way, that you should be worrying about possible injunctions. Let us be quite clear about 'front' zone. (This is where the confusion, referred to in the opening paragraph of this chapter, comes in.) It does not mean – and is therefore rather a misnomer – the area nearest to the front wall or window of the room. It means the last 25% of well lit area.

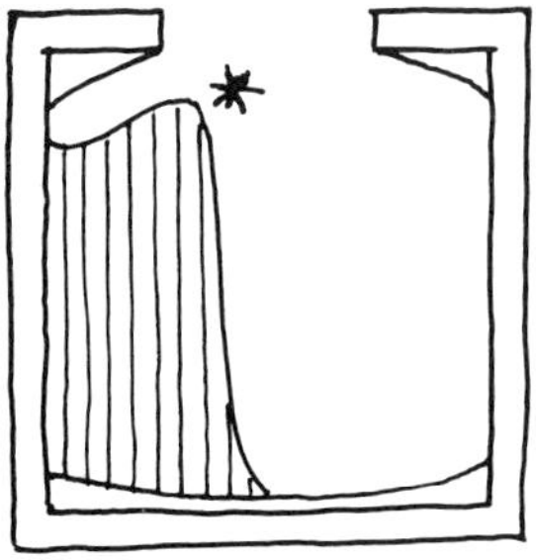

60%, SAY, REMAINS TO 0·2% S.F.
– NO ACTIONABLE INJURY.
ALL LOSS "MAKEWEIGHT."
* N.B. NEARNESS OF LOSS TO WINDOW IS IRRELEVANT.

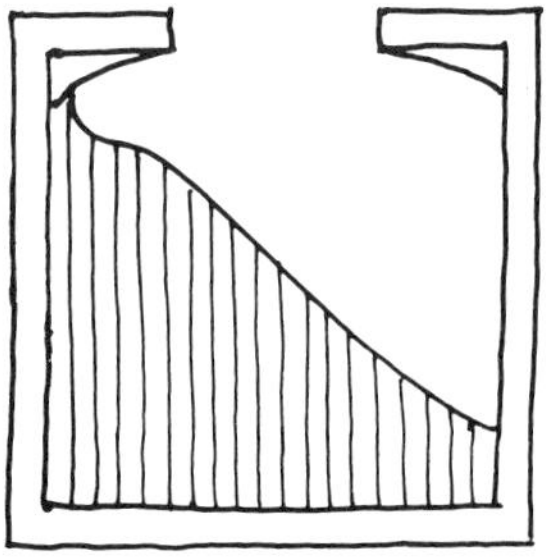

40%, SAY, REMAINS TO 0·2% S.F.
– ACTIONABLE INJURY
SOME "1st", SOME "2nd" LOSS

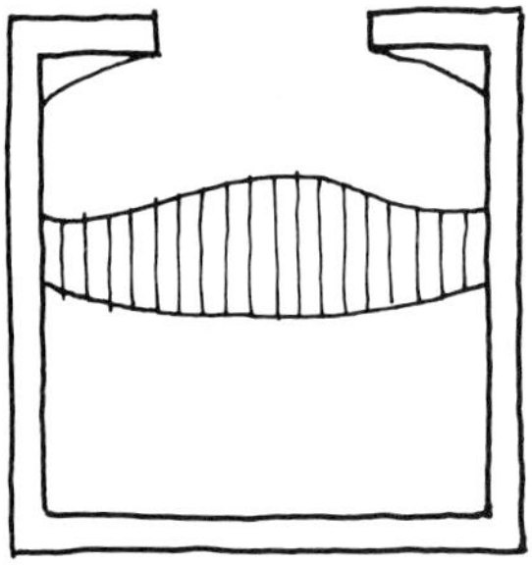

30%, SAY, REMAINS TO 0·2% S.F.
– ALL LOSS "1st"

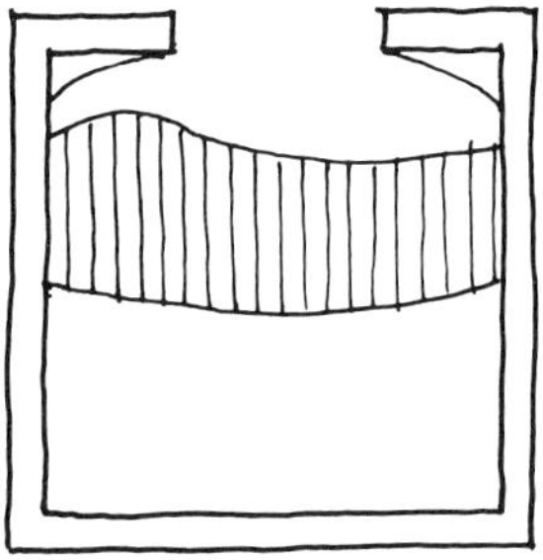

15%, SAY, REMAINS TO 0·2% S.F.
– SO SOME "1st," SOME "FRONT LOSS.

If you had a very small window, giving a narrow shaft of light right to the back of a room, it could be that any obstruction to that window would produce front zone loss – against the back wall. Now let's return to the mathematics.

Adding together the figures we have produced above gives a figure of 110 square feet, expressed in the equivalent of first zone areas: hence, efz. When many rooms in one building are affected, some may suffer losses which would not be actionable in themselves, since the room remains well lit: two such are illustrated in the table. Those losses nevertheless have to be taken into account as makeweight, and their areas are divided by four. I always value staircases and lavatories in commercial buildings as makeweight. If the contrary is argued, ask whether a tenant expects to pay the full figure per square foot for such areas. Now we can proceed to evaluate the loss in money terms.

The method of valuation evolved through many meetings and discussions between leading consultants, and in 1971 the three most

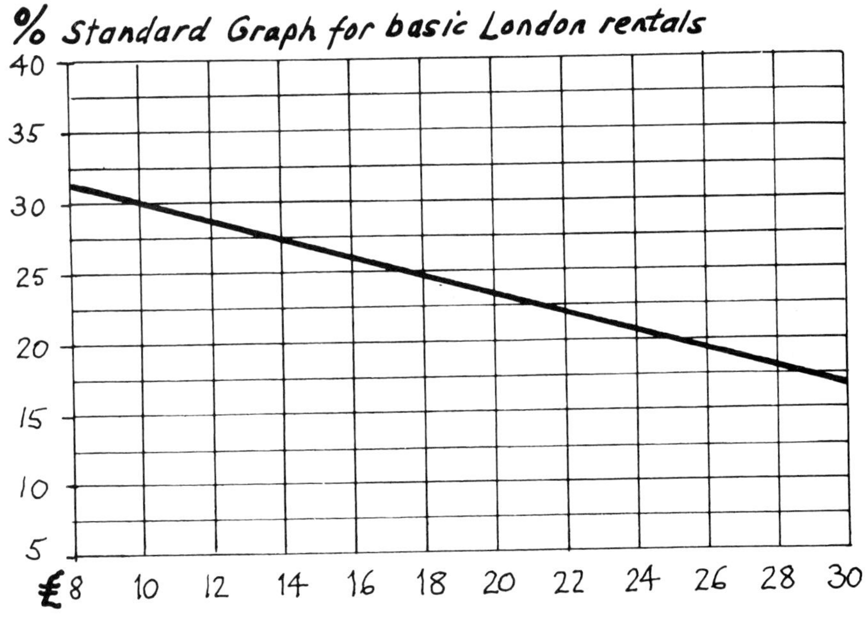

This graph is more or less agreed by all today's leading rights of light practitioners as showing the percentage of rack rental value per square foot attributable to natural light

eminent of their time, Bryan Anstey, Keith McDonald and Eric Arnall, sat down and codified their view, which included the breaking down of areas set out above. They also agreed that the value of light as a proportion of rent varied according to the importance of position and other factors so that, as a general rule, the higher the rent, the lower the percentage attributable to the light. A graph was drawn up which enabled you to read off a figure for light against any rental figure.

Unfortunately, the advent of what one might call 'high tech' rents during the 1980s began, in many people's opinion – and certainly mine – to distort the light values obtained from the graph. So many other factors were now inflating rents, such as the availability of computer channelling and big, open, dealing floors, that even applying the lowest percentage shown in the graph produced a figure which quite clearly exceeded the true value of the daylight as such.

A new consultants' conference was called, at which the

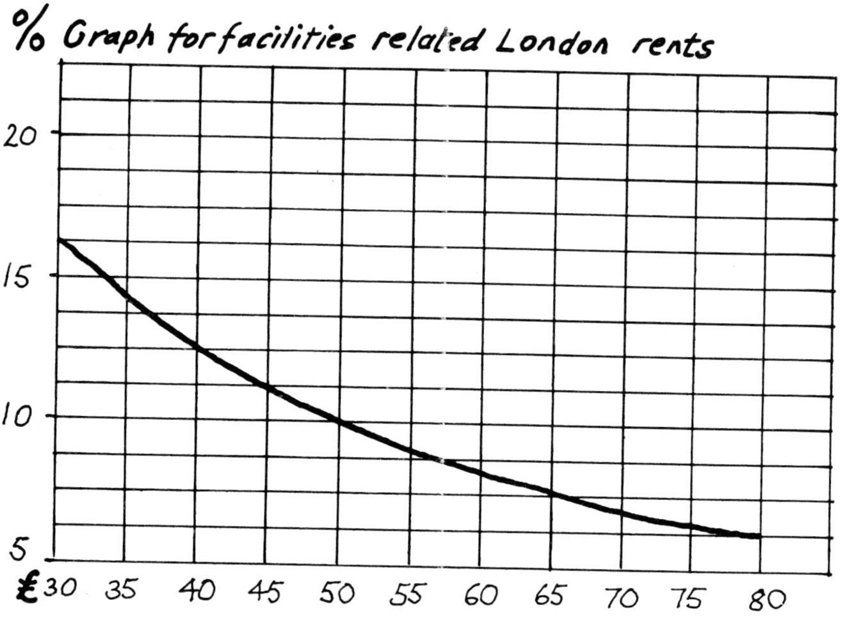

This graph indicates that, however high the rent being paid for 'high tech' facilities, the amount of the rent attributable to light is never more than £5

successors of two of the original three were present, and the third's successor was kept informed since he was unable to be there; three of the newcomers to the sport were also present. All agreed that for London rents even in excess of £50 per square foot, no more than £5 should be adequate to represent the value of the light. Furthermore, no premises were now available at the lowest figure shown on the old graph, and so a new starting point was chosen. For areas outside London, similar principles should be followed, but the wide variation in provincial values, coupled with the narrower range of rents in any one of those centres, made it difficult to settle upon one particular scale or graph, although a tentative one can be produced.

At the time of writing, the new graphs have not been 'formally' adopted in the way that the old one was, but it is pretty certain that something very close to them will be, so I will risk producing them here for your delectation, including one which indicates the light value of £5 whatever the 'high tech' rent.

All that is left for you to do now is to agree upon the rental

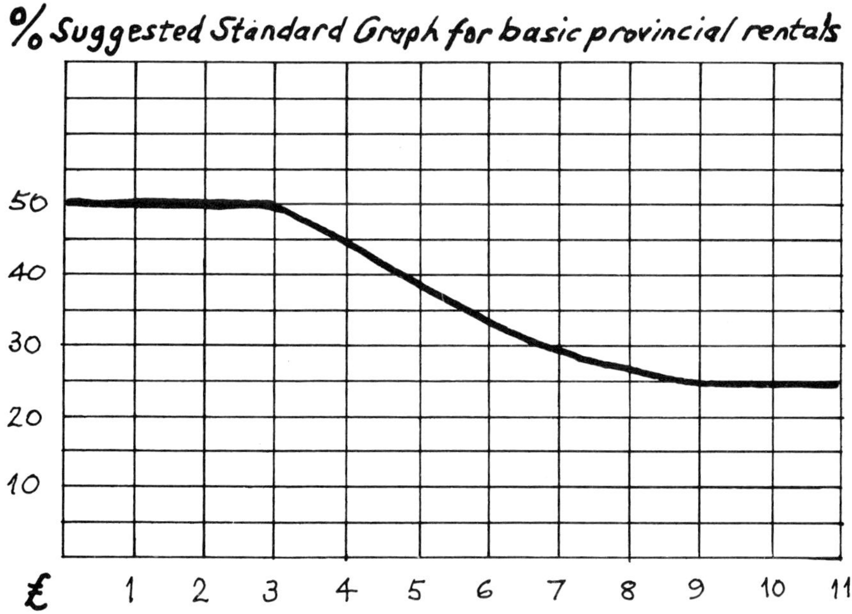

This is a very tentative graph indicating the sort of percentages which might be used to derive the value of light from provincial rents

value, and the rest follows in the mechanical steps set out above. Agreeing rental value is not difficult, especially when a variation of a pound or so is only going to make a difference of pence in the light value. When I have been called upon to give an impartial decision on an injury, which can happen quite often – there is a certain area of the city where I am advising four or five owners, who are all developing in a way which affects at least one of the others, and all have agreed that I should simply tell them who owes whom what – if the money involved is likely to be substantial, I call in valuers for each of the parties and let them agree first on the rental value, after which I apply my manipulations. I also ask for valuation advice when I feel out of my depth on a case where I am only acting for one side, and this can happen very easily in cities where I have no first-hand recent knowledge of rentals. You will probably also welcome advice on capitalisation, since the last task is to arrive at a capital figure for the injury, which you get by multiplying the light rental value by the efz and then by the appropriate YP.

Rights of light consultants always value injuries on the basis of a freeholder in possession, and that is all that really matters to the servient owner: that is the figure, plus fees, that he is going to pay out. However, there may be several interests in the dominant tenement which all have to be appeased, depending upon how their leases are worded, and whether the landlord has reserved all rights of light to himself. The developer may be asked for several cheques, but they should all add up to the number he first thought of.

As this is a chapter, not a treatise, on valuation, I am going to have to assume a certain degree of knowledge on the part of my readers. If they don't understand the concept of YP, they must either read a general book on valuation, or ask someone to explain. In order to apportion the 'freeholder in possession' sum between the said freeholder, the long leaseholder, and the occupying tenant, you will now need a copy of *Parry*. Using the single rate table, no allowance for tax, and choosing the percentage column appropriate to the YP you have used in capitalising the compensation in the first place, you can read off the multipliers to be used according to the period up to the next rent review.

Let us look at a typical example. You have agreed an injury of 300 square foot efz, and a light value of £5, producing an annual figure of £1,500. You then agree a YP of 18 to produce a capital figure of £27,000. There is an occupying tenant with 3 years to go to his next rent review, and a head lessee with 27 years left without review. The argument is that at a review (for any lessee) the rent will be assessed in the light (joke) of the prevailing circumstances, and so each is only affected until the next review.

Find the column in *Parry* closest to 18 YP, which is 5.5%, of which the perpetuity figure is actually 18.1818. Divide your capitalised total by 18.18. You may ask why we didn't multiply the £1,500 by 18.1818 in the first place. The answer is because we probably didn't have *Parry* open at the time, and having agreed upon a figure of 18 YP and its resultant capital product, the paying-out side is not going to be keen to agree a higher figure now just in order to simplify the calculations. Nobody is going to lose by this method, at least not in relation to the capital sum agreed in the first place. So, I repeat, you divide by 18.18 to produce a slightly different annual figure. If you use a calculator, you can divide by 18.1818, but I prefer working in my head, or long hand on paper, so I'll cut my division to two places of decimals. The answer is £1,485 as near as makes no difference. We may have to juggle a pound or two later to make everything fit.

Looking down the 5.5% column to 3 years, we find a multiplier of 2.6979, which I will call 2.7. That times £1,485 equals £4,009 and is the occupier's share. Next we find the head lessee's terminal date of 27 years, and a multiplier of 13.8981 which, by now you will not be astonished to learn, I will round off to 13.9. You must deduct the 2.7 already paid to the tenant, and then multiply £1,485 by 11.2, producing £16,632. Theoretically, you should now be confident that, since £16,632 plus £4,009 equals £20,641, the sum of £6,359 is the freeholder's share. However, I always carry out the last calculation to make sure I've done the others correctly, and we'll do so here.

We know that the perpetuity figure is 18.18, so we deduct the 13.9 already distributed, leaving 4.28 which, times £1,485, produces £6,356. We've therefore got three pounds to play with from our various simplications, so we'll give one to each party. The tenant gets £4,010, the head lessee £16,633 and the freeholder £6,357. I repeat that if you use a calculator the figures will come out more accurately – or only wrong by a factor of ten. The long division and multiplication is good for the brain, however, and quite accurate enough. I might say, in parenthesis as it were, that the ability to do sums in your head can be very valuable. I was once chatting idly to a District Valuer about a compulsory purchase when a chance remark he made indicated that he was thinking of offering a higher price for some properties than I was thinking of asking. I was able to work out in my head a number of figures which, when multiplied together produced a number slightly in excess of the amount he appeared to be thinking of, and then allowed myself to be beaten down to his original idea. I'm sure that it wouldn't have looked half so convincing if I'd had to do my back working on a calculator in front of him. The client, by the way, who had been perfectly content with the figures I was intending to ask for, manifested no great signs of gratitude for the considerable increase with which I presented him.

What is the position if the freeholder has reserved all rights of light matters to himself? One very distinguished authority argues that, as he will suffer no damage until the date of his reversion, he should only get the compensation deferred: the £6,357 in our example above. With all due respect (which, as my father was fond of pointing out, can mean none; but, in this case, means a lot) to my colleague, I disagree. Theoretically, in my opinion, the lessee will have reduced his bid if he is going to have to take the kicks of loss of light without the ha'pence of compensation. The landlord will therefore already be in receipt of less money than if he had allowed the tenant to participate in any prospective loss, and so he is entitled to receive the whole sum (in the example) of £27,000. I agree that, in fact, this calculation is unlikely to have been done by the prospective tenant – though it's quite possible that the landlord will have done it – but the theory is correct.

You may by now be rather confused, so I will set out again, but very simply (and not in the same order) the steps to agreeing rights of light compensation:

- agree the rent, and then the value of the light in that rent, probably using the agreed graph;
- agree the appropriate YP;
- measure the areas of room, old well lit, new well lit, and thence the loss;
- apportion the areas of loss according to degree of seriousness, and reduce them to equivalent first zone (efz) in square feet;
- multiply your three factors together: efz, rate and YP;
- if necessary, apportion the capital compensation between the various interests.

The valuation of domestic property is in many ways more difficult. Values per square foot are not available, so one has to take an empirical view, based on capital values. The value of a particular room has to be considered and staircases, for example, which may be of little value in commercial premises, can be the sole means of communication between important parts of a dwelling, often used in twilight hours, so that daylight is very important indeed. Lavatories and bathrooms are of slight importance, in daylight terms. You may have some considerable difficulty in agreeing the value of a domestic injury, but let us assume that you eventually do.

All you have to do now is agree upon a suitable form of release, which can be as simple as that illustrated in *Permissive and restrictive deeds* or as complicated as a full-blooded legal document, and then send in your bill: which leads me to my next chapter. But before closing this one, I should perhaps say a little about 'parasitical' damages and 'blackmail'. It is a well-established legal and practical principle, well illustrated in *Carr-Saunders* v *McNeil Associates* (which see), that the developer, or servient owner, may have to pay over the book value of damages in some cases: this can be for losses of other amenities not in themselves actionable, or for losses of light in other rooms which have not actually reached the actionable level. This is because the dominant owner's basic right is to an injunction, and once you have been injured at all, if you are deciding whether to allow yourself to be bought off, you will have in mind more than the mere actionable injuries. After all, you would prefer to be left with your light, and your adversary must bear that in mind when making offers of settlement. Sunlight, view, and ambience are rather hard to quantify and you may have to pluck figures out of the air. However, you may also have to agree figures for losses to some rooms, which are not actionable in themselves, but which have to be taken into account in arriving at a total of compensation acceptable to the injured party. These are usually added into the efz calculation at the makeweight rate.

Blackmail is not a dirty word in rights of light circles. It is a short and convenient way of describing the fact that, in commercial cases where both parties know perfectly well that the dominant owner could certainly obtain an injunction if he put his mind to it, the servient owner is going to have to pay well over the odds in compensation. The figure can range from about one and a half times the book value to almost any number you care to think of: half of the extent of the development value which could not be achieved without the dominant owner's acquiescence should be regarded as the maximum – and that not frequently attained. Rumour reaches me of a case in which well over the total development value was paid to be released from a very restricting covenant. I don't understand the mathematics of this; if true, and I suspect dark doings on one or possibly both sides. Within my own knowledge is a negotiation where a property company asked for such an extortionate figure in blackmail damages that the developer retorted that he could buy the company for that figure, let alone the particular property in their portfolio which he was affecting.

So now on to a more pleasant subject.

Chapter 13

Fees

If I had charged any percentage fee which you can imagine on the major jobs with which I have been concerned, I should now be living a life of comfortable affluence and devoting all my time to writing books on abbeys, castles, and Venice, while doing the odd consultancy of national importance just to keep my hand in. However, that would not have been fair to my clients, since I should have been vastly overpaid for the amount of work I actually had to do on those projects – though perhaps not if you take the analogy of the surgeon who was asked to itemise his bill of 100 guineas for an appendectomy. He replied: to taking out appendix, £5; to knowing how to take out appendix, £100. Be that as it may, I always charge on time actually spent on a case, inflating it if I have had to drop other matters and rush around at the urgent request of a client, and cutting it down for private individuals to whom the charges might otherwise be a considerable burden. It is not unknown for me to make no charge at all to a deserving person who has no hope of recovering the costs from the other side.

If I am asked to estimate what the fees on a job are likely to amount to, I usually point out that rights of light are always a matter of action and reaction, and that my fees will largely depend upon how difficult the neighbours are. It won't even necessarily depend on how much compensation has to be paid out, because effectively rebutting a spurious claim can take just as much time and effort as settling a justified one.

I find that the only equitable way to charge is on an hourly rate, with a minimum fee for taking a case – higher for a servient owner than a dominant owner, because it takes more time and trouble to advise the party doing the development than it does to estimate the likely effect on an injured building. When the fees for the time spent exceed the minimum fee, I simply total up the hours for myself and my assistant (charged at a lower rate, for form's sake, not because he is less valuable than me) and bill them accordingly.

I should point out that I reckon that I'm the best there is, and that nobody else should be charging more than me – if I find out that they are, I put my charges up. Very, very few people should charge as much as I do, and I think that no-one would dispute that no other assistant is worth anything like as much as mine. That is because my assistant, Michael Cromar, worked for my father before me and has therefore an enormous amount of experience, unequalled by anyone now in practice. Strictly speaking, he isn't my assistant, because he has a separate practice and his services are available to all who can afford him and for whom he can find time. What I mean is that all my technical assistance is provided by his firm, and is therefore charged for accordingly, but it's easier in general terms and when talking to clients to speak of 'my assistant'.

Travelling time is always difficult to deal with. If I travel the length of England to a job, which I frequently do, then on an hourly basis my charges would always exceed my minimum, even to a servient owner, but I generally reckon to get more enjoyment out of travelling to Scarborough or Exeter, and therefore I usually stick to the minimum fee, especially if I can dispose of the whole job in one visit, and sometimes I can combine it with another in the same direction, which saves a lot of time on both.

I'll always be prepared to fit a site visit into a trip taken to distant parts for primarily pleasurable reasons, such as visiting abbeys, castles, or parrots, and therefore not even to think about charging for the travelling – but the client has to be lucky enough to find me in his vicinity at the right time.

Sitting through court or enquiry proceedings is exceedingly unproductive, and I always beg clients – and their lawyers – to have me in attendance for the minimum time. However, if I am compelled to sit through three days of proceedings in order to give twenty minutes' evidence, I charge for three days. In fact, I have been known to threaten to charge more if I'm not cross-examined.

That's the demanding part of giving evidence and, as long as you really know your stuff, should be the most enjoyable. Unfortunately, for some reason or another I frequently give my evidence unchallenged. I would like to think that it was because my evidence was unchallengeable, or that the other side was afraid of my replies, but it may be because they thought I wasn't worth the expenditure of shot. It always worries me when it happens.

I am reminded of a rather two-edged anecdote of which my father was rather fond – although I think he only saw one of the edges. He used to try to leave some devastating riposte for cross-examination, and would dangle a lure for counsel in his evidence in chief. On one occasion in a planning enquiry he did so, and counsel did not rise to cross-examine. 'Have you no questions for Mr Anstey?' enquired the Inspector. 'No, thank you' was the reply. 'I've seen Mr Anstey defend himself before.'

Well, back to fees. How much and how you charge is really up to you, but I do think that you should try to do a little social justice in your charging. And don't forget: if you charge more than me, I'll increase my fees – so you might let me know if you intend to do so.

Chapter 14

Planning: personal and public

I suppose that I chose the title of this chapter for its alliteration, but what it really means is that satisfying the planners as to the merits of your proposals – or the demerits of your neighbour's – is an entirely different matter from sorting out any common law rights between you and your adjoining owners. (And in London, the same goes for party walls.) Some councils, very helpfully, make a point of stressing this in a note accompanying planning permissions, but an enormous number of my jobs are accompanied at some stage by the bleat of the developing owner: 'Next door can't be affected; the council have approved it'.

I know that I have complained at several points in this book about the lack of certainty in some areas of the law, but compared to planning the certaintyfulness is terrific – as a certain schoolboy might have remarked. There used to be excellent guidance available to planners on the subject of *Sunlight and Daylight*, in an eponymous booklet published by the DoE in 1971. Unfortunately, very few planners seem to have read it accurately or in full. The booklet draws a very clear distinction between the standards to be looked for in planning new buildings and those to be applied when considering redevelopment or the insertion of new buildings into existing contexts. I devoted a whole article in *Property Management* (Vol 3 No. 4, 1986) to this failing of local authorities, to which I would refer interested readers, but I will make the main points again here.

The first and most important point to make about *Sunlight and Daylight* is that its authors stress, in the second paragraph of the work, that 'The advice given is not mandatory. The criteria put forward do not constitute a set of overriding rules. . . . In the last resort decisions must be based on common sense and judgement'. This advice is expanded elsewhere in chapter 1, but I get the impression that many local authority officers skip the Introduction and get straight down to the guidelines, and then adopt them uncritically without heeding the reservations they have skipped.

Chapters 3 to 5 set out the criteria, and chapter 7 explains the use of 'Daylight Indicators' which can be used to test whether a building receives enough daylight to meet the planning requirements. No-one practising in the field of daylighting should fail to read and grasp the whole of these chapters, if only to be able to understand the language which the planners will be speaking. However, he should also read, very carefully, chapter 6, which I can only assume has been missed out of the copies sold to local authorities, so great is the ignorance of it among such bodies.

Here follow some relevant quotations from chapter 6. 'Interested parties cannot automatically expect that any proposed buildings should stand clear to the extent indicated by the block spacing criteria.' (Those are the guidelines set out in earlier chapters.) 'The protection of an existing building should be based on an assessment of what difference the proposal would make to it, i.e. to a comparison of "before" and "after" conditions at important places. . . . This "before" and "after" assessment can often be made by an expert on-site judgment without measurement.' (I am fond of pointing out immodestly that this is what I do.) 'If measurement of daylight is necessary the daylight indicators should not be used.'

Up to this point, one can have had a certain sympathy with authorities who have adopted the criteria as more or less mandatory standards which must be met. After all, councils are entitled to take their own view of standards which should prevail in their locality. Now, however, any sympathy is lost by those planners who insist on using daylight indicators in the face of blunt instruction to use other methods. What are the methods recommended by the DoE? First and foremost, the Waldram diagram. The only criticism offered is that it is complicated and takes time, but since daylight practitioners are going to be accustomed to using it, that's not going to be a problem for them. In theory, then, you should be able to use Waldram diagram studies to prove to a local authority either that your client's building is affected in such a way that planning permission ought to be refused, or that the proposed building causes so little change in the before and after stakes that permission should be granted. But don't count on it.

Sunlight is another matter entirely. You know by now that there is no right to sunlight (not yet, anyway), but planners do consider the subject. I should emphasise that sunlight is really only relevant to residential buildings, and the criterion intended for guidance on development of new estates and the like is that all points 2 metres

(I'm afraid that's how they express it, but they mean 6 feet 6 inches) above ground level on buildings facing anywhere south of east and west should have the possibility of three hours' sunlight on March 1st. There are refinements of calculation including, strangely, the fact that due west counts but not, by interpolation, due east: it seems that you have to face 1° south of east to count. The above statement is good enough as a general guide, and you should read the original in any case.

My complaint here again is that rigid observance misses the point and can be very unfair to the infiller or the loft conversioner. If a property nearby already gets less than three hours' sunlight on March 1st, is a neighbour to be absolutely barred from causing a loss of five minutes? In some localities the answer, apparently, is yes. If the property gets no sunlight on March 1st, should the neighbour be permitted to cloud all the summer sun? If you take the same narrow view again the answer ought to be yes. The reason why those questions and their answers appear silly – and I hope they do – is that you are applying a design criterion for new properties to what *Sunlight and Daylight* calls 'the existing building problem'. The criterion is meant to test whether you have planned the siting and orientation of a proposed building in such a way that it makes the best use of available sunlight.

By far the best method of studying the effect on sunlight in existing situations is the use of the Sunpath Diagram. It was impossible for the DoE to commend this system since it was developed as a result of the publication of *Sunlight and Daylight* in answer to the need demonstrated therein for considering 'before' and 'after' sunlight. Writing in the *Architect's Journal*, in June 1973, Peter Burberry demonstrated his development of the Waldram diagram, by which it was possible to measure the effect at any date and throughout the day of any proposed alteration in the skyline upon the sunlight potential of any spot. I owe my knowledge of this to an architect whose name is now lost in the mists of time, who kindly sent copies of the articles to Michael Cromar soon after their publication. If he reads this, he should know that he is not forgotten, even if his name is.

I have successfully used the Sunpath Diagram in actual cases to prove that, for example, though there is a loss on March 1st, well over three hours' sun will remain throughout five months of the summer. The method is not nearly as well known in planning or design circles as it ought to be, and I commend it to you.

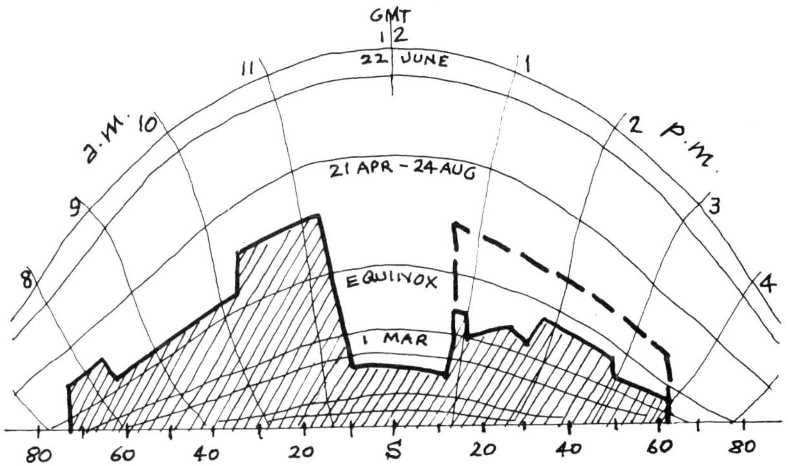

A sunpath diagram.
Hours of the day are shown horizontally, and time of year vertically. In the case illustrated, the point chosen for study receives less than two hours' sunlight on March 1st, and a neighbour proposes to add an extension which has no effect on that date. It will, however, take away three hours' sunlight for about two months of the year. I think that such a change may be relevant, but do the planners?

To return to the private sector: I repeat that it is no defence to a neighbour's complaint to say that you have planning permission. I have said it so often that I can't remember whether I've already said it in this book, but in any case it bears repetition: I have known permission refused on daylight grounds for developments which were harmless in common law terms, and I have known permission granted for proposals which were injunctable.

If you are faced with objections on daylight grounds to a development, whether or not the complainant also objected to the planning authority at the time of the application, you must investigate his complaints on the common law lines set out earlier in this book. If he has a valid objection, you may even have to redesign your building to meet it, and go back to the planners for an amended permission. You will be very unlucky if they are unsympathetic to a change which has been forced on you, and they may even approve the alteration on the nod.

Rather than rewrite the whole of the above chapter, much of which is still true, I must add a section on a new publication from the Building Research Establishment, which is designed to supersede

Sunlight and Daylight. As there had been an even earlier publication, *Daylight and Sunlight*, I suggested that this one should be called *Light and Sunday*, as the only untried combination, but the powers that be opted for the more prosaic *Site layout and planning for daylight and sunlight. A guide to good practice.* This still stresses, though perhaps not enough, that it contains guidelines, not rigid rules. Unfortunately, I think that it is all too probable that local authorities will seize on those guidelines which they can understand and practise – some of them are far from easy – and use them rigidly.

Angular limits are given for restricting development which might affect daylight, and percentage losses are suggested as being permissible for both daylight and sunlight. A flow chart is provided, which asks the rather curious opening question: 'Is there a rights of light injury?' How many planning applicants – or authorities – are going to know the answer to that?

Astonishingly, the Sunpath Diagram is not incorporated, but an inferior – in my view – system is suggested for assessing sunlight losses. This is really a great opportunity missed.

The booklet is too recent for any real knowledge of its working and effect to be available, and it may well be modified by time and experience. You will need to buy a copy and study it, however, if only to know how planners are going to look at your proposals. If this book reaches a third edition, I may have some more useful comments to make.

Chapter 15

How to be a rights of light consultant

In the preceding chapters I have tried to give you the background of law and practice that you need to learn in order to be able to advise people about their rights in light matters, whether vis à vis the local council or their neighbours. In the Appendix which follows (to knowing how to write Appendix, £?) I set out a number of leading cases, a thorough knowledge of which will enable you to sound very impressive indeed. What else do you need to set up your plate as a consultant?

A long apprenticeship seems to be the best training, since the three foremost experts today all served alongside their predecessors for a considerable period. If you can't find such an opening, go very gently at first, until you're sure that you can cope with the more complicated sort of jobs.

If you are to be able to deal with a job involving more than one window you must start practising doing Waldram diagrams now, long before you're going to need to do them in a hurry for an impatient client. Don't forget that you'll have to do a separate diagram for every point you study and, until long practice improves your estimation of where to start, you may need to take several points before you get one close to the 0.2% line. Although I've given you a rough idea of how to do a Waldram study, a practical demonstration from a real expert is much the best way to learn this tricky art. And then, as the man said when asked the way to Carnegie Hall: 'Practise, practise, practise'.

Learn to count brick courses fast and accurately. The first is necessary because you don't want to be caught measuring up the dominant owner's premises so that you may assess the potential injury to be caused by your development. Practise this skill on your own building: dash outside, measure up the elevation by brick counting and guesswork, and then check it by rod and line.

Don't let clients rush you into an opinion. Often they will go round the building with you and demand to know ('We're exchanging contracts tomorrow') whether there's any risk of an injunction. There's only one answer to that question if they want it quickly: 'Yes'. You need to think carefully about the size of the injury and the nature of the dominant property before you can answer, and the evidence needs time to mature in your head.

Don't be afraid to give clients the answer they don't want to hear. If someone wants to be told that their light is injured, and you bow to their pressure, you may be allowing them to embark on costly litigation from which, in fact, it is your duty to deter them. They'll blame you quickly enough after losing in court.

Do hedge your opinion with the necessary legal qualifications, but don't be afraid, when necessary, to advise your client to disregard the hedge – like Peter the Great.

Be consistent. Don't argue one way for a developer and another way for a claimant. Be sure your sins will find you out. People often send me extracts from my writings to try to prove me wrong on certain matters, and I have to explain to them the distinction between the generality in the writing, and the particular matter under discussion. And I mean just that. You can't write one thing and then attempt to argue the contrary to suit a particular client.

Don't attempt to run before you can walk, and don't even walk when you're still a crawler. I was once instructed in a negligence case against a surveyor who, when asked specifically if he was able to deal with rights of light, replied with a categorical affirmative. He wasn't.

Now that you've assimilated all the wisdom offered in the earlier chapters, and taken in all the dos and don'ts of this one, there is only one thing left to do. Read the Appendix to put the final polish on your learning, and then go out and be a better consultant than I am. If, as the Duke of Plaza-Toro so quickly added, possible.

Appendix
Some interesting cases

Rights of light law depends heavily upon leading cases, and therefore the discussion of many points during the course of this book has been larded with reference to such cases. I think that it may, however, be helpful as well as interesting for the reader to know a little about some of the more important cases, and I have also covered one or two in which I have had a personal involvement and about which I can therefore speak with even greater authority. When I got down to it, there turned out to be a considerable volume of case law which could bear reporting, but I hope you won't find it too much. You don't have to read this section if you find it boring: most of the legal principles which arise from these cases should have been incorporated in the text you've already got through.

The last report is a warning not entirely to trust even leading cases.

Dent v *Auction Mart Company*, 1866

In reading up this case, I have learned that it was concerned with premises immediately opposite the office where I first worked in the City, in 1952. Messrs Dent's building stood on the corner of Kings Arms Yard and Tokenhouse Yard, and the Auction Mart Company had bought properties further south in Tokenhouse Yard, which they were proposing greatly to enlarge.

According to one of the plaintiffs' witnesses, the result would be 'to place the staircase windows . . . in a dismal stagnant well', among other dire effects. The defendants admitted that there would be some effect, but said that it would be very limited, and that they were quite willing to minimise it by using white enamelled tiles.

Some heavy forces were mustered for the battle. There were actually three plaintiffs, who all had one QC in common, but the Attorney-General appeared as leading counsel for Dent & Co, who took the lead, and the junior was a Mr Kekewich (presumably the one who later became a judge and, since it is a fairly uncommon name, probably an ancestor of a girl with whom I was at University). The case was heard by Sir W. Page-Wood, V-C, who took as his basis for the law to be applied, the words of Best C.J. in *Back* v *Stacey*, 1826, where he said: 'In order to give a right of action and sustain the issue, there must be a substantial privation of light sufficient to render the occupation of the house uncomfortable, and to prevent the plaintiff from carrying on his accustomed business on the premises as beneficially as he had formerly done.' The Vice-Chancellor proposed substituting 'or' for 'and' in the middle of that quotation, but otherwise completely accepted it.

An ingenious interpretation of beneficial carrying-on of business had been put forward by the defence: that if you did not lose a customer or client, you had suffered no loss. This novelty was rejected by the court. It was also argued that because Dent's had said that they would take £2,000 to shut up and go away – an astronomical figure at the time – they had given up their claim to an injunction. I have often advanced this line of argument myself, likening the situation to the case of George Bernard Shaw and the actress. He asked her if she would sleep with him for £10,000, and received a favourable response. He then offered £10 and was haughtily asked: 'Sir, what do you think I am, a prostitute?' 'I thought we had settled that question' replied G.B.S., 'and were now only haggling about the price'. I still think this must be true if, for example, you ask for two or three times the proper amount of damages, but the court's view in Dent was that a figure absurdly over the top really meant that money was not an adequate remedy. Page-Wood reiterated that a neighbour should not be forced unwillingly to take compensation if he preferred to maintain his rights.

In his judgment, the Vice-Chancellor disposed of a great number of arguments that had been put up by the defence. They had wanted less consideration for town houses than country ones; he felt that the law was the same, even if country windows were less likely to be obstructed. They argued that other people made do with less light; he held that the plaintiffs' easement did not entitle them only to other people's bare minimum. The Auction Mart Co said that Dent's should have enlarged their windows; Page-Wood answered that it was not for the Defendants to tell the Plaintiffs how they were to construct their house. Another of the plaintiffs had used venetian blinds; the judge said that the occasional closing off of light does not mean that the dominant owners should be permanently deprived of it.

Finally he came to the matter which makes this case a favourite of mine. Obviously a very forthright chap, Sir W., and I take great pleasure in quoting him. 'Then, lastly, there was the suggestion of glazed tiles – often made and never listened to by the Court. A person who wishes to preserve his light has no power to compel his neighbour to preserve the tiles, or a mirror which might be better, or to keep them clean . . .; and, therefore, it is quite preposterous to say, "let us damage you, provided we apply such and such a remedy".'

The defendants' QC had urged appointing a jury to view the scene of the crime, but Page-Wood thought (and I hope his successors are noting this carefully) that 'the benefit of a view . . . is a good deal exaggerated. If the jury could have had an opportunity of viewing the premises as they existed a year ago, and could be taken to view them as they exist now, the view might be very serviceable. But as it is . . . when a jury view premises as they are, without the slightest knowledge of what they were before, they may be influenced by the remark which was pressed upon me, but which I think is of no value whatever, namely, "Why, there are plenty of people in London who have not so much light as you have" '.

There are other drawbacks, too, and I am sure he was alert to them, such as changing light conditions from day to day: note that he suggested the use of comparisons a year apart – implying the need to have at least similar weather for the experiment.

Accordingly, Dent & Co won their injunction.

Angus v *Dalton/Dalton* v *Angus*, 1881

This case has nothing whatever to do with light, but everything to do with rights to it. The reason for this apparent paradox is that it concerned the other most popular kind of negative easement, the right of support. Consequently, the judges in the case kept alluding to analogous light cases. I have learned a lot by reading a full report of this case in the Queen's Bench Division and Court of Appeal, over 80 pages of it, and I am going to pass on some of those gems to you. Some of it is history, and could perhaps be incorporated by rewriting a passage I have already written, but I think that I prefer to present it to you where I found it: embedded in *Angus* v *Dalton.*

The facts were very simple. Angus altered his premises 27 years before the events, so that his factory was more or less supported by a chimney stack which took the ends of some main girders. Dalton pulled down his property (somebody else's, actually: he was only the contractor) and did some excavation, leaving the stack standing on a pillar of clay which soon collapsed, bringing the whole factory with it. All the argument was about whether the stack had acquired a right of support during those 27 years, since there was no way the servient owner could have stopped the acquisition, except by pulling down his own property and letting Angus fall down sooner. There was some subsidiary discussion as to whether client, contractor, or sub-contractor was liable, but that was very brief and need not concern us.

I must admit that I don't follow just how cases were managed in those days. It seems that a judge heard the case with a jury, and then it passed to a bench of judges for the next stage. Anyway, Lush J. heard the case originally, and then also delivered the first judgment of the Bench. He drew attention to the similarity of support and light, but pointed out that support was the more onerous, because of the difficulty of preventing acquisition of rights.

While examining how rights were acquired, Lush J. remarked: 'I cannot help thinking that the revolting fiction of a lost grant may now be discarded.' One hundred years later, his wish has still not been granted. Another point of discussion he referred to was the difference of opinion between the Exchequer Chamber (whoever they were) and the Court of Queen's Bench as to whether the Statute of Limitations ran from the time when the wrong was committed or the time the damage actually occurred. As we know, that one hasn't finally worked itself out yet, either.

Having examined all the cases, he decided that the factory was 'ancient', and found for the plaintiffs: that they had a right of support.

Cockburn C.J. gave the second judgment, and said that the case was of 'very great importance as regards the law of easements'. He was the historian of the party and, after also deploring the fiction of the lost grant, examined the way in which prescription had developed. Different rights were, apparently, referred back to different dates. Until 1235, most rights had to be shown to date from before 1100. By the Statute of Merton, 1235, writs of *right* (it goes without saying that I don't understand half of this: I'm just passing it on, undigested) were limited to the time of Henry II, 70 years previously; writs of *mort d'ancestor* were not to pass the last return of

King John from Ireland, a period of 25 years; and writs of *novel disseisin* were not to pass the first voyage of the King into Gascony, 15 years before. In 1275, the Statute of Westminster fixed new periods of limitation. Writs of *right* were limited to the time of Richard I, 1189; *novel disseisin* stayed where it was in Gascony; but writs of *mort d'ancestor*, *cosinage*, of *aiel*, and of *entry* were limited to the coronation of Henry III, about 58 years.

As I had surmised, nobody then thought it worth while changing the date of prescription, even when, in Henry VIII's time, some of the other dates were altered. James I's reign brought another statute affecting limitation for possessory action, and there the law stayed until the time of William IV, not one of England's most memorable Kings, and the Prescription Act, 1832, which we all know and love. So much for history.

Cockburn C.J. and I have at least one thing in common: we both think that the Prescription Act could have been better worded. (Why doesn't Parliament do it now, I wonder? Any legislators reading this book are invited to discuss the matter with me.) The Lord Chief Justice went so far as to describe it as 'this strange and perplexing statute'. I feel a lot better about my difficulties with it now. He thought, and I think, that it would have been much more helpful to have had a series of fixed periods of prescription, and no other claims to be allowed except on production of positive proof of title – presumably written. Farewell the lost grant and time immemorial. He concluded that 'by this roundabout and ... somewhat clumsy contrivance' (referring to the Act) 'twenty years' use or enjoyment was rendered a presumption *juris et de jure*'. So now you know.

Later on there occur references to decisions at *Nisi Prius*, my only knowledge of which comes in the immortal quotation:

And that *Nisi Prius* nuisance who just now is rather rife,
The judicial humourist: I've got him on the list.

Anyway, after much citing of cases, he concluded that as Dalton (or rather, his client the Commissioners of Works and Buildings) had never granted a right of support or assented to Angus's construction, the right was open to be rebutted, and he found for the defendants. Fortunately for us, Mellor J. concurred with the Lord Chief Justice in nine lines.

The case then went to the Court of Appeal. (By the way, you don't have to read all this if you don't want to, but I've often wanted to know more about what lay behind those oblique references to leading cases that one gets in the text books, so I've got hold of them, read them, and made some extracts for your benefit if you want them.)

Thesiger L.J. (doubtless an ancestor of the famous representatives of the clan today) also dwelt upon the fiction of the lost grant, though he was by no means as opposed to it as some of his fellows. After examining the remarks of the L.C.J. in the court below, in a sentence rife with double negatives, he agreed that the right of support was a bit different from all others, except perhaps light. Although we are only in the middle of his judgment (after 13 pages), he then summed up the question and effectively gave his decision. 'Can it properly be said, then, that the difficulty or practical impossibility of obstruction in the case of the easement of support for a building by soil is such as to place it at common law in an entirely different category from other easements, and to render it subject to any real legal distinctions? I think not.'

I wish I had time and space to examine all the interesting variants on support which were discussed, touching the difference between unloaded soil and houses erected thereon, and the effect of chopping away supporting pillars when the house was already above mining operations, and the distinction to be drawn when the land excavated was not adjacent, but perhaps I'll write a book on support some time.

Having reviewed the authorities, Thesiger L.J. was satisfied that, for over 100 years, the courts had been of the opinion that a right of support could be achieved by proof of uninterrupted enjoyment for 20 years. Accordingly, he gave judgment for the plaintiffs, unless the defendants wanted a new trial. This is another bit of old-fashioned legal proceedings that I don't follow.

Cotton L.J. gave the next decision, and argued that 20 years' enjoyment did not raise an absolute right, but a presumption which could still be defeated by such matters as the incapability of the grantor. The fact that there was no grant (which all admitted) did not defeat the presumption. He pointed out that enjoyment still had to be open. (Much to my surprise, no-one quoted *nec vi, nec clam, nec precario* in so many words.) He was not sure that the mode of enjoyment had been known to the servient owners, and thought that Lush J. should have left that matter to the jury. For that reason, he, too, thought that the defendants could have a new trial – presumably on that point only, the Court of Appeal having laid down the law on the right of support.

Finally, Brett L.J. delivered his speech. He pointed out that, despite their differing views on the proper verdict, the Queen's Bench had agreed on a great deal: that the right to lateral support for buildings is not a right of property; it can exist as an easement; it can only have its origin in a grant; that it's not covered by the Prescription Act; and that 20 years' enjoyment after knowledge by the adjoining owner was enough to secure the right – in the absence of other defects in the right. This question of knowledge was knocked about a bit, and has come up in other cases, including light ones, where a greater than ordinary amount of right was being claimed. It was certainly discussed in *Allen* v *Greenwood*. The servient owner has to be aware of the right which is being relied on, and I suppose it comes under the general heading of *nec clam*.

Brett L.J. summed up the differences by saying that Lush J. thought that, as a matter of law, after 20 years' enjoyment without physical obstruction, the right could not be defeated by the absence of a grant, or lack of knowledge by the defendant, or mere verbal objection. The other judges thought that the 20 years was only *prima facie* evidence of a grant, but that if there was doubt about it, it should be left to the jury, while if there was certainly no grant, judgment should be for the defendants.

He dismissed the claim, still being run by Angus's side, that support was a natural right in property – which would have given them a win by a knock-out. In dealing with the next question, he pointed out that if a man erected a house with windows on the very extremity of his land, he needed no grant to do so. He only needed a grant if he wanted those windows to remain unobstructed. (At this point – in 1881 – he quotes *Gale on Easements*.) By 20 years of imposing this additional burden on next door's land, he can achieve this putative grant, and the case with support is like unto it. The additional burden of the weight of the house prescribes for its right over time, so that on the day the house is built, only the land on which it stands has a right of support, whereas when it has been up for 20 years the house itself is entitled to support. He agreed with all the points on which the Queen's Bench were agreed, and then turned to the points on which they differed.

Lush J., in the opinion of Brett L.J., went too far in his 'bold step' of holding that 20 years' enjoyment in itself confers a right. The jury should be allowed to find whether there was a grant – lost or otherwise. Brett seized on Lush's use of the words 'revolting fiction' to support the view that there must be a matter for the jury to decide. Use from time immemorial means that a jury must find for prescription; use for a lesser length of time is only evidence on which they can make their own decision.

Brett L.J. then reiterated all the points on which he and the Queen's Bench were agreed, and then held, for himself: that if there was no evidence led about the impossibility of the existence of a grant, the jury had to be directed to find a lost grant; if there was doubt as to the notice to the adjacent owner or the existence of a grant, it should be a matter for the jury; and if there was not sufficient evidence of the building having existed for 20 years, or if there was positive evidence that there was no grant, then the defendant was entitled to win. On the evidence, there was no grant, therefore he would uphold the Queen's Bench.

Three-all, therefore, after the most exhaustive examination of the law, but the plaintiffs were left in possession of the field – unless the defendants should opt for a new trial. I have not yet learned whether they did.

Well, there we are. An enormous commentary on a case which has limited relevance to the matter in hand, but which has, as I have already said, always intrigued me. And anyway, I wasn't going to waste all my effort in ploughing through it on your behalf, without writing my own version of it.

Shelfer v *City of London Electric Lighting Company*, 1895

This case also, of cardinal importance in dealing with rights of light, had nothing to do with light at all. In fact, the Lighting Company had caused damage by excavation for the foundations of their plant, and were continuing to cause annoyance by vibration and noise from it. However, nuisance is nuisance, and the law is the same when considering whether to grant an injunction or to award damages in lieu. Mr Justice Kekewich (he who had been junior counsel in Dent's case?) had awarded damages, and the plaintiff appealed.

A substantial part of the case in the Chancery Court was concerned with whether the Lighting Company were exempt from an action because of their statutory position, but this need not detain us. Having held that the defendants could be – and were – liable, Kekewich J. found that they had damaged the Plaintiff's premises so as to make them less comfortable, but that the profits of Shelfer's business had not been interfered with, and that there would be great inconvenience if the Defendants' business was stopped – among

1,500 or so buildings which they were supplying with electricity were the Bank of England, the Mansion House and the Guildhall. Accordingly, damages were a fair compensation, and no injunction ought to be granted.

In the Court of Appeal Lord Halsbury gave the first judgment. He was of the opinion that, without Lord Cairns' Act, there would definitely have been an injunction. That Act, however, had changed the legal position, and the question was: to what extent? In his view, the well settled principles indicated that an injunction was still appropriate in the present case, since otherwise someone like the Lighting Company could force a neighbour to sell his rights.

Lindley L.J., in giving the second judgment, instanced *Imperial Gas Light and Coke Co* v *Broadbent*, 1859, where the Lord Chancellor had said that damages 'cannot sufficiently indemnify the party who is injured', which made an injunction obviously necessary. It made no difference, in Lindley's view, whether the defendants were doing work of benefit to the public, and his only doubt about the effect of Lord Cairns' Act was whether it applied in *quia timet* actions. (That doubt no longer exists: see *Lyme Squash.*) It was clear that the Act did not intend to turn the Court of Chancery into 'a tribunal for legalising wrongful acts'. He was of the opinion that damages should only be awarded instead of an injunction under 'very exceptional circumstances. I will not attempt [he added] to specify them or to lay down rules for the exercise of judicial discretion'. A.L. Smith L.J., as we shall see, was less hesitant about doing so.

In the third judgment, A.L. Smith was quite certain that jurisdiction existed to award damages or an injunction. The difficult question was: which? In answering his own question he made several very important observations, from which I have extracted the following quotations.

'Many judges have stated, and I emphatically agree with them, that a person by committing a wrongful act . . . is not thereby entitled to ask the Court to sanction his doing so by purchasing his neighbour's rights, by assessing damages in that behalf, leaving his neighbour with the nuisance, or his lights dimmed, as the case may be . . .

'In my opinion, it may be stated as a good working rule that –

(1) If the injury to the plaintiff's legal rights is small,
(2) And is one which is capable of being estimated in money,
(3) And is one which can be adequately compensated by a small money payment,

(4) And the case is one in which it would be oppressive to the defendant to grant an injunction:-
then damages in substitution for an injunction may be given.

'There may also be cases in which . . . the defendant by . . . for instance, hurrying up his buildings . . . has disentitled himself from asking that damages may be assessed in substitution for an injunction . . .

'An injury to . . . light to a window in a cottage represented by £15 might well be held to be not small . . . whereas a similar injury to a . . . large building represented by ten times that amount might be held to be inconsiderable. Each case must be decided upon its own facts; but to escape the rule it must be brought within the exception.'

It is clear not only that A.L. Smith had rights of light well in mind, but also that he regarded an injunction as being very much the normal remedy, and damages the exception. Shelfer's case, in his judgment, was clearly not a case for damages, but for an injunction to restrain the continuance of the existing nuisance.

Whatever may be the practice today in commercial cases, even when quite large injuries are in issue, the law is quite clear, as was to be firmly reiterated in *Pugh* v *Howells*, 1984 (which see). If his easement is threatened, a man's basic right is to an injunction.

Colls v *Home and Colonial Stores*, 1904

The case is put this way because Colls brought the action in the House of Lords, but he was the original defendant, as he (I suppose it's probably 'they': perhaps the forerunners of Trollope and) had sought to put up a building in Worship Street, and the Home and Colonial Stores had objected. The High Court had rejected the claim, but the Court of Appeal had granted a mandatory injunction to pull the premises down. Colls appealed against this to the Lords, who unanimously upheld the appeal.

The Lord Chancellor, Lord Halsbury, gave the first judgment, and quoted approvingly *Yates* v *Jack*, 1866, in which Lord Cranworth said that the right was to 'the enjoyment of the light without reference to the purposes for which it has been used', and also Malins, V.C., in *Lanfranchi* v *Mackenzie*, 1867, when he held that a person could not, even by using the dominant premises for 20 years for some special purpose requiring an extraordinary amount of light, acquire a right to some extra degree of light. But see *Allen* v *Greenwood*, a bad decision, later.

Another matter touched on was the question of alterations and their effect on the easement. The Lord Chancellor agreed that the non-user of a prescriptive right to light, or its partial use, did not detract from the right, but he felt that it was wholly unreasonable if a dominant owner could alter his building so as to impose an instant new burden upon his servient neighbour.

The main question to which Lord Halsbury addressed himself was whether the diminution of light suffered by the Home and Colonial justified the award of an injunction. The facts were that the room complained of was a long, deep one, with no windows at the rear, so that even a very moderately sized building opposite was bound to affect the penetration of light to the back of the room, even though a normal sized and shaped room might have been unaffected. Relying on the finding of fact by the High Court judge that the building's effect on the light did not amount to a nuisance, he reversed the Court of Appeal's finding in law that the change was injunctable.

Lord Macnaghten, giving the second judgment, considered whether the law had been changed, except as to the period of enjoyment necessary to prove a right, by the Prescription Act of 1832, and cited with approval judgments both before and after the passing of the Act which said, respectively: that it was necessary to 'distinguish between a partial inconvenience and a real injury to the plaintiff in the enjoyment of the premises'; and that for it to be actionable, the diminution had to be one which made the premises 'to a sensible degree less fit for the purposes of business or occupation'. He was of the opinion that the test was unchanged.

A most interesting observation he made was that instead of viewing the premises, a judge might well rely on the report of a competent surveyor appointed by the court. There is still a great deal of merit in this suggestion. It is very rarely that competent rights of light consultants disagree as to the facts of an injury: cross-examination is usually (but not always) directed at their opinion of the severity of the effect. Instead of wasting two chaps' time in court on a largely futile exercise, why not return the expert witness to his original function, that of assisting the court; let him report the facts and let the lawyers argue about the effect.

In his opinion Lord Davey, with whom Lord Robertson agreed, also held that the test of nuisance was unchanged by the Prescription

Act, and remarked that the purpose for which the dominant owner had thought fit to use the light did not affect the question. Lacking the Waldram diagram, whch was not invented till later, he thought it perfectly proper for surveyors to employ the 45° rule as a good working guide, even if it was not a rule of law. (As we have the Waldram diagram, this is no longer true of the 45° rule, but the principle that a method which surveyors find to be of good practical assistance in determining the effect should be accepted, must still, surely, apply.)

Lord Lindley felt that it was unreasonable to allow no change in a dominant owner's light, or nothing would ever get built. He touched on the relevance of light from other directions, and thought that it should be disregarded if it could be legally interrupted. But it is his closing paragraph which, in many ways, is most interesting. He regretted the lack of a definite rule applicable to all cases, and said: 'First, there is the uncertainty as to what amount of obstruction constitutes an actionable nuisance; and, secondly, there is the uncertainty as to whether the proper remedy is an injunction or damages'. I couldn't have put it better myself; I'm not so sure about the next sentence, however. 'But, notwithstanding these elements of uncertainty, the good sense of judges and juries may be relied upon for adequately protecting rights to light on the one hand, and freedom from unnecessary burdens on the other.' Well, I suppose that if anyone has to have faith in the law it ought to be the House of Lords, but if the lower courts are infallible, why do we need the higher ones?

Smith v *Evangelization Society (Incorporated) Trust*, 1932

A lot of what had been said in *Colls* was reiterated in this case, with some useful additions. Additions are what caused the problems, as well. An open space had gradually been walled and roofed, and skylights were put in and taken out again. In 1931, the defendants blotted out the light to a replacement eastern window. The celebrated Percy Waldram gave evidence for the plaintiff.

The whole case really turned on the skylights. If they had not been removed by the plaintiff, they would have provided enough light for the area which lost light through the obstructed window. The plaintiff argued that light from above was quite different, and ought not to be taken into account. The judge disagreed, and the plaintiff appealed.

The Master of the Rolls agreed with the judge's findings, quoted extensively from *Colls*, and rejected the appeal. Lord Hanworth said that you had to look at the premises at the start of the prescriptive period, and that the dominant owner was not entitled to claim an increasing use over the twenty years.

In the second judgment, Lawrence L.J. said that skylight was not analogous with reflected light, but was as good as, if not better than, side light. Romer L.J., too, quoted from *Colls*, and pointed out that to lose light is not actionable in itself. Both judges therefore agreed with the Master of the Rolls in dismissing the appeal.

Since skylights are very difficult to obstruct, and can light a large area, you should always keep your eyes open for them in areas where they might be relevant.

Sheffield Masonic v *Sheffield Corporation*, 1939

This is really the key case on light from alternative sources. Sheffield Masonic Hall had windows facing north and east, all of which were ancient, and Sheffield Corporation began building a substantial art gallery and library to the north, which would obstruct the light to those windows. The Corporation argued that this didn't matter provided that the eastern windows, which faced an open space behind which was a low building, continued to provide enough light to the function room for ordinary purposes.

Maugham J., in the Chancery Division, reviewed the arguments of the defendants, which could be summarised as 'First come, first served'. They should be allowed to build, they said, throwing the whole burden on to the eastern windows, and if someone came along later wanting to develop the open space, that was the later comers' hard luck. The judge felt that this gave rise to injustice, and that both servient owners would be placed under an uncertain obligation to the dominant owner. I think he was wrong, as it happens, because I think that to take the facts as you find them when you begin work on site is much easier than hypothesising about what might be built in front of the alternative windows.

However, the judge went on to take the other view, that: 'At the moment when the right is acquired by the plaintiff company in respect of both of the two windows on the north and the two windows on the east the nature of the restrictive obligation imposed upon people facing those two (did he mean four?) windows is that they will not so build as by their joint action to cause a nuisance to the plaintiff company'. In other words, the Corporation could only build to a height which allowed a similar building to be erected on the land to the east which, when both buildings were considered jointly, would still allow enough light into all the windows taken together to be sufficient for the ordinary purposes of its user.

The judge then went on to cast doubt on the value of expert evidence, the Waldram diagram and the measurement of light at table height, saying that a building 10 feet away was much more injurious than one 60 feet away, even if they took away exactly the same amount of light. These are all propositions with which I would be prepared to argue.

For the rest, this case can almost be summed up in the words of Arthur Hugh Clough:

> And not by eastern windows only,
> When daylight comes, comes in the light,
> In front the sun climbs slow, how slowly,
> But westward, look, the land is bright.

Cory v *CLRP*, 1954

This case is an archetypal City (of London) rights of light case and Mr Justice Upjohn's judgment set out the legal considerations very clearly.

CLRP were about to redevelop 9–11 Billiter Square, when William Cory and Sons brought a *quia timet* action to stop them, that is to say, one in which the plaintiffs 'fear lest' something might happen, rather than allege that it already has. It happened that the windows of the rooms of the major directors of the company on the first floor looked out at the site, together with those of several senior managers on the ground floor.

The judge said how well established the Waldram diagram was, and explained about the 'grumble line' – a term which is sometimes used for the 0.2% sky factor contour. He does not seem fully to have understood the conditions in which that 0.2% will have represented an actual one lumen contour, but he appreciated that the actual amount of light would vary with the seasons and the time of day. He also accepted the 50/50 rule (which is explained in Chapter 1), but warned that notions might change.

The figures put forward by the experts did not all agree, but the judge thought that the differences were not significant. Much more important was their agreement that loss of light to a room already ill lit was more serious than if the room began by being well lit. The rooms in question had previously been 50%, 45% and 40% well lit (or thereabouts) and it was proposed to reduce those areas by about 25%, 17%, and 17% respectively. (The figures are given in the law report as percentages of the well lit area: nowadays one normally talks of percentages of the whole room. I would not be absolutely sure that the figures were not of the latter kind.)

The judge then turned to considering whether damages or an injunction was the appropriate remedy. The argument had been put to him – as it nearly always is by defendants – that in reality the plaintiffs would suffer no loss, such was the demand for offices in that area. He rejected this approach, saying that the plaintiffs were not interested in dealing in offices, but in maintaining the light for the senior men of their organisation. There would be a real change in their conditions if the development were permitted and so, although the defendants might be placed in some difficulty by having to change their plans, get a new planning permission, and by having already fabricated steel for the proposed building, he felt that an injunction was the proper remedy.

In passing, Upjohn J. referred to the movement of a partition which had occurred during the prescriptive period, and which had altered the prescriptive effect in two rooms.

He held, quoting *Colls*, that the right was to a shaft of light coming through the window, and that internal alterations, unless they were for extraordinary purposes, do not affect the dominant owner's right. I am not happy with this view, as it is too easy for the situation to be drastically altered by the dominant owner, and I think that a well argued case, in which this is the main point, should result in the judgment that prescription must relate to one set of circumstances.

Ough v *King*, 1967

The issues in *Ough* v *King* can be very simply summarised. Mrs Ough claimed that her light had been injured. Bryan Anstey gave evidence that just over 51% of the room remained well lit. The County Court judge visited the room on a grey afternoon in February and decided that the room was dark. As I always point out when writing or talking about this case, the Crystal Palace would be dark in those circumstances. He therefore held that the light had been injured, and that the 50/50 rule which had been accepted in *Cory* v *CLRP*, (which see) was not a rule of law (which we knew) and shouldn't therefore be slavishly adhered to (which may be regarded as unhelpful).

The Court of Appeal held that the judge was entitled to come to that decision. At least Diplock L.J. said that the 50/50 rule was still a convenient rule of thumb. Let us hope that the courts may continue to be all thumbs.

Metaxides v *Adamson*, 1971

By an odd coincidence, I, the son of the expert witness in this case, was telephoned by the son of Mr Metaxides in search of some plans, just before I came to write this note of the case. I did see the property in question, but only in a very subordinate role.

The architects to the parties had made what purported to be a party wall award, but as the houses were in Richmond the 'award' had to be adopted by the principals by a deed of rectification. This gave the right to Mr Metaxides' predecessor in title to open certain windows. This was duly done by Mr Metaxides, and Mr Adamson then erected a trellis in front of the windows, and started growing pyracanthus and wistaria up it.

Mr Metaxides sought a declaration that he was entitled to light through three windows, and an injunction restraining the plants. The judge held that the grant of the right to open the windows implied a grant of light to them and, accepting absolutely the evidence of Bryan Anstey, held that the kitchen had been seriously injured, the bedroom less so, and the lounge not at all.

Unfortunately, Mr Metaxides had been a bit slow in bringing his action, so that Mr Adamson had not been offered a chance to move his plants and establish them elsewhere. Accordingly, the judge decided against an injunction but ordered an enquiry as to damages.

Allen v *Greenwood*, 1978

You can find a whole article by me on this case in the *Estates Gazette* in January 1979 which, if it had no other merit, at least succeeded in introducing one reader to the charms of Asterix the Gaul.

This case was, in my opinion, rightly decided in the lower court and wrongly reversed in the Court of Appeal. Over the years, the question of a right to an extraordinary amount of light had been much argued and, said *Gale* in the thirteenth edition, 'finally decided in the negative in *Ambler* v *Gordon*, 1905'. Early in my career I came across a case, the name of which I cannot remember, in which a family had matched fine silks in Soho for over 200 years, and yet were denied any greater than usual level of illumination by right of law.

Mr Allen owned a house in Rochdale which had had a greenhouse since 1940. In 1974 Mr Greenwood proposed to erect an extension to which Mr Allen objected, and later began to park a caravan immediately alongside the greenhouse. Then he began to erect a fence on the boundary, about 6 inches away from the greenhouse, and eventually extending to 18 inches above the eaves of the structure.

Vice-Chancellor Blackett-Ord found that, although the light had been affected, there was still plenty of light to do ordinary things, including reading a book. He remarked that 'there is no evidence that the owners of the servient tenement . . . knew the precise use which was being made' of the light in the greenhouse to grow tomato plants from seed. This 'precise' knowledge was a point discussed in *Dalton* v *Angus* (which see).

The Court of Appeal, having heard no argument to the contrary, held that a greenhouse was a building within the meaning of the Prescription act, 1832, and referred to an express decision to that effect in *Clifford* v *Holt*, 1899. The matter came down, therefore, to the question of whether the appellants could justify a claim to a 'specially high degree of light'. The respondents argued that it wasn't really the light which was making the difference, but the rays of the sun, which were a different matter entirely.

Goff L.J. started his examination of the law with *Colls* v *Home and Colonial Stores*, 1904 (which see), to establish the basic principle that enough light must be left for the ordinary purposes of a building. He was of the opinion that the ordinary purposes of a building which happened to be a greenhouse would require, and be entitled to, a greater amount of light. He also held that the servient owner would know the sort of uses to which greenhouses were put, and that they therefore did have sufficiently precise knowledge.

Goff L.J.'s decision may be summarised as being to the effect that it was absurd if the plants had enough light to read their growing instructions, but not enough light to grow by. He dismissed the argument about the warmth of the sun, in the particular circumstances of this case, but said that at some future date, perhaps with reference to solar heating, it might be necessary to distinguish between daylight and sunlight. I agree, but I think that those elements did get themselves confused on this occasion. The two other Lords of Appeal agreed with Goff L.J. without adding anything of any great importance.

It is notable that in this case, as in one or two others of importance, there does not seem to have been any expert evidence. I have visited the site and, although I did not carry out a detailed inspection, I am of the opinion that Mr Greenwood's house already overshadowed Mr Allen's greenhouse to some extent, and that the effect of the fence was not as great as believed by Mr Allen and the Court of Appeal. On a second visit, I found that Mr Greenwood, who refused to talk to me, had parked his caravan alongside the greenhouse again.

Easthope v *Gawthorpe*, 1983

This is an unreported case which illustrates the application of the Sheffield Masonic principle, and also the dangers that may lurk in the wording of various covenants.

Mr Gawthorpe started to erect a substantial addition on the site of his garage, and Mr Easthope objected that it would darken the light to his living room, and to the bedroom above it. The expert consulted by Mr Gawthorpe was of the opinion that enough light would (or could, in the case of the bedroom, since there was a substantial item of furniture blocking the way) come to the rooms from other windows.

There was a complication in that there was a covenant in the deeds, saying that neither party (or any others on the estate) should do anything which might be or grow to be an annoyance to his neighbour. The lawyers for the defendant thought that if the injury was not an actionable one at common law, then this clause would not be infringed.

The matter was heard in the High Court before the judge, Finlay J., who had been counsel for King in Ough versus that gentleman. The expert for Mr Gawthorpe was terrified to discover that evidence for Mr Easthope was to be given by the man who had devised the daylight indicators, but fortunately the judge preferred the Waldram diagram method of calculation, saying that it was more suitable for intricate cases.

The plaintiffs naturally argued that the light from the

alternative, smaller, window was not adequate and that, in any event, one should allow for a similar obstruction to its light. The judge held that the obstruction had to be a realistic possibility and that, as two long gardens and a road intervened between the window and any likely building, it could be considered to be free from risk of darkening. So we (sorry, I mean Mr Gawthorpe) thought we had won. But soft, what light through yonder window breaks? It is the covenant, and Mr Easthope is the beneficiary.

The judge decided that an injury need not be actionable for it to be an annoyance within the meaning of the deed, and therefore Mr Easthope was entitled to succeed. He didn't think, however, that the injury warranted an injunction and so he awarded damages.

Richard Rogers, the architect, was less lucky with a similar covenant. There the judge awarded an injunction despite the fact that there was certainly no rights of light injury. He held that the mere presence of the proposed construction would be an annoyance to the neighbour. Fortunately, Mr Rogers' brilliant consultant was able to design a complicated structure, with planes meeting at all sorts of interesting angles, to such effect that it not only gave Mr Rogers all the space he needed but will no doubt come in time to be considered a work of architectural genius and ascribed to the great man himself. After all, that has already happened to some extent in respect of the chunk cut out of the south west corner of the Lloyds building.

It seemed to me a little harsh that, having succeeded in three-quarters of our case, Mr Gawthorpe should have to pay all the costs, but he did.

Pugh v *Howells*, 1984

In striking contrast to some people involved in leading cases, Miss Pugh was very hospitable when I asked if I might come and look at her house, but I am sorry to say that I am far from sure that she even suffered an actionable injury. If she did, however, then there is – paradoxically – no doubt that the Court of Appeal were correct in awarding her an injunction instead of damages. But let me tell you about the case.

For many years, the possibility of an extension had been looming over the Pugh family, and they had resisted it at every turn, with Miss Pugh taking the lead. Eventually, she noticed that Mr Howells had started taking down the lean-to extension at the rear of his house, which formed part of the same terrace as the Pughs' house. The latter already had a two-storey rear extension which had been constructed in about 1900. Miss Pugh's solicitors wrote and told the Howells that they would resist any building which affected the light to their rear room and kitchen, and over one bank holiday weekend, the defendants rushed up the extension to roof level.

Miss Pugh brought proceedings for an injunction in the County Court, and produced technical evidence which I regard as worse than useless. No doubt her consultants had done their best, but they relied on that most misleading of bases, light levels measured in lux or lumens within the room. On their first visit, they attempted to compare Miss Pugh's existing light with that of the next house up the hill, which happens to be affected by her existing extension. On their next visit, in completely different weather conditions, they measured the light now received in Miss Pugh's rooms, after the Howells' extension was up. It is clear from their reports that the consultants recognised the deficiency of their system, but still they used it and attempted to extrapolate from their readings a scientific conclusion as to the effect on the Pughs' light.

The judge found that the Pughs' light had been injured, and awarded £500 in damages. At the time, the house was probably worth about £10,000. Miss Pugh however is a doughty fighter, and she did not want the money: she wanted her light. She consulted her barrister again, and he produced an excellent piece of reasoning as to why, given the judge's findings of fact, she should have obtained an injunction. Impressed by this (as I was, when I read it recently) she invested her savings in an appeal. Brave woman! I don't think I would have done.

Counsel argued, and the Court of Appeal accepted, that all four tests laid down in *Shelfer* (which see) had to be passed before the court should exercise its discretion to award damages in lieu of an injunction. The judge had come to the conclusion that it was 'not a serious nuisance', and had paid no regard to the unhelpful behaviour of the defendants, both in dealing with correspondence and in hurrying up their building.

Waller L.J., giving the first judgment, said that the judge had relied on reading p392 of *Gale on Easements* (that was in the 14th Edition: it's page four hundred and something in the 15th), and had said that although the Howells deserved no sympathy, he would only have ordered the work to be pulled down if he had thought that it was a serious nuisance. Waller pointed out that in his judgment on Shelfer, A.L. Smith had said that even if the four tests were passed, a defendant might by his conduct rule himself out of getting away with damages. Even though he, Waller, was not certain that the four tests had been passed in the present case, he would still have been reluctant to upset the judge's conclusion, but since Howells' action clearly came within A.L. Smith's exceptions, he would allow the appeal and substitute an injunction.

In the second judgment, Fox L.J. opened by saying: 'This is a case in which there was a significant interference with the rights of light'. Later on, he stressed that the judge had not found that the injury was small, only that it was 'not a serious interference'. He, too, was mindful of the defendants' behaviour, and concurred in granting the injunction.

When I went to see the properties, the upper storey had been taken down, and only a single storey extension – though much larger than the old lean-to – was in place. I therefore had to guess at the original extension, but it was my impression that about 55%–60% of the Pughs' two affected rooms would still have had 0.2% sky visibility. There is no doubt that they would have suffered loss, but not to the degree normally considered actionable by the courts. Miss Pugh was, I think, very lucky in her choice of consultants, and, with more merit, her barrister.

The lesson of the case, however, does not lie in my view of the facts, but the court's view of the law. Shelfer's case was emphatically restated, and it was made very plain that reckless servient owners cannot expect any sympathy from the law. A man's basic right is still to an injunction: damages are the exception.

Lyme Valley Squash Club v *Newcastle-under-Lyme BC*, 1984

I disagree with the decision in this case, and with the amount of damages awarded, but I have been told by the defendants' expert witness that my grave doubts as to there actually being an injury are justified but wrong. In Michael Pitts' own words 'the window head is set comparatively low and . . . the internal depth of the room . . . is unusually great in relation to . . . window head height . . . which results in an unusually low angle . . . from the back of the room at working plane height to the window head'. But all this will be meaningless to you, without having learned the basic facts. However, I wrote an article (entitled, with extraordinary wit, *Lyme Squashed*) in which I cast doubt on the actual effect, and Michael wrote to put me right on that subject. It is the least important part of the case, whose other aspects are examined below.

A company which proposed to build a squash club bought a piece of land from the local authority, which retained land on three sides of the site. In the contract of sale was a condition that the purchaser was not to obtain any easements over the retained land which hindered its development, but this clause was inadvertently omitted from the actual conveyance. It was accepted that the clause in the contract had not been deliberately inserted to allow for development: it was just in a standard form which happened to be used. At the time, it was expected that the area would be used as a car park – and, as a matter of interest, I gather that it still is being so used, six years after proceedings began.

At a later date, the council decided to allow some land to be developed for shopping, and the squash club objected that their light would be affected. Naturally, the council relied on the contract and the club on the conveyance. As it happened, the club-house had been at least partly built before the conveyance was executed, so that, if the words of the conveyance were held to govern, there would be an implied right to an easement to the windows. The judge held that, because no-one gave any thought to the 'reservation' clause, it was right for him to go behind the contract, and find for the squash club.

In his judgment, Blackett-Ord V-C seized upon the words of Goff C.J. in *Allen* v *Greenwood* (which see) which, in my opinion, had already overdeveloped the meaning of the judgment in *Colls* (which see) and said that a right to light was to that light required for the beneficial use of the building which received it. As these cases follow each other, it would seem that the rule that there is 'no special right to light' is fast disappearing. Although he was not impressed with the plaintiff's valuer's evidence about the importance of light to a squash club lounge, the judge accepted that the light would be affected by the proposed building (which, as I explained at the outset, had seemed unlikely to me, based on the facts I then knew) and that the plaintiffs ought to have damages, not an injunction, if the shop development went ahead.

Unfortunately, the defendants had offered to do some sort of landscaping for an area outside the windows, and were lured into costing that at about £10,000. The judge obviously thought that this was a useful figure, and so fixed upon it as the amount of damages. The order was made in a rather strange form, to the effect that if the defendants paid the money by a certain date, the injunction granted would not prevent them from building in accordance with the plans before the court. I believe that the development has not yet occurred; I don't know that the money was ever paid; if so, it will have been a somewhat Pyrrhic victory for the squash club.

Carr-Saunders v *McNeil Associates*, 1986

This case illustrates the limitations of the dictum that light receivable from other sources must be taken into account, and also the application of the principle of parasitical damages. It also demonstrates the importance of speaking clearly when addressing the judge. Mr McNeil is a film producer, and urgent business had called him away. At one point, the judge asked why he wasn't present, and counsel replied that he was on location in Spain. The judge, mishearing the word as vacation, rather crossly asked what the defendant was thinking about, to go on holiday when an important case affecting him was being tried.

McNeil Associates and their architects had fallen into the common trap of believing that since they had planning permission and were really only bringing their building more or less into line with their neighbours, there was nothing to worry about. Unfortunately, they were building in Shorts Gardens, behind which lurks Neals Yard, the buildings of which were only a short distance away from the back of the development. Carr-Saunders objected that the light was being taken from the windows at the rear of his premises, which had been a warehouse, with no windows on the ground floor, open plan first and second floors with windows back and front, and a very high roof which Carr-Saunders had recently converted to provide living space for himself.

The first floor was still an open space, but the second floor was newly converted into small consulting rooms for an alternative medicine consortium (to which I had, quite coincidentally, recently turned in despair to seek relief for a long-standing digestive complaint). There was no doubt that the light to the two rooms at the rear had suffered, but McNeil's side (I among them) argued that the new conditions were not prescriptive, and that in the old open plan there would still have been 50% of the room well lit, since the windows on the opposite side were not likely to be obstructed and continued to provide plenty of light.

There were a number of subsidiary arguments, but the essence of the judge's decision on this point was that a reasonable man might want to divide a 20 foot wide building into several rooms (even though Carr-Saunders had not done so when he occupied the second floor, nor in his new eyrie) and that the light from the opposite windows had never reached the areas which were now losing their light. I'm still not sure why this last point is relevant, since the ability to rely on other windows is surely bound to mean that some areas are lit by one window and some by another, and you must consider the overall effect. However, there was no doubt that the cubicles had been seriously affected, and the judge was saying, in effect, that you couldn't rely on windows 20 feet away to contribute to the lighting.

This brought us to the question of damages. There were two valuations before the judge: that of the plaintiff's architect, which did not follow any known precedents and reached the astonishing total of £24,000; and that of the defendant's expert, which had been prepared in accordance with the principles set out in *The Valuation of Rights of Light* (written by the witness), and which amounted to £3,000.

The judge unhesitatingly accepted the figure of £3,000, but pointed out that damages were an equitable remedy, and that in deciding to forgo his right to an injunction, Mr Carr-Saunders would also have had in his mind the loss of sunlight (slight, but admitted by the defence) and the general deterioration in the ambience. For that reason he awarded a further £5,000, making £8,000 in all.

It would be dangerous to try to take a general rule from this case, but a rule of thumb multiplier of two and a half times the 'book' damages to forgo a possible injunction can sometimes be helpfully used. I have known cases, however, where one and a half was a better figure, and others where two and a half was laughed at for its inadequacy.

The auld widow woman

Not every leading case should be taken at its face value. I have seen counsel's opinion on one particular matter which solemnly stated that proof of injury was not always necessary for the recovery of damages, and he cited a certain case in which £50 was awarded. I have never seen that particular case quoted anywhere else, but lest you should come across it somewhere, I set out below the true facts (with fictitious names and probably embroidered a little) as received by me at my father's knee. It was an Irish case.

That distinguished rights of light expert, Bryan Anstey, had been consulted, through solicitors, by an Irish bank. He had carefully examined the drawings of the bank's extension, and its relation to the premises next door, had come to the conclusion that there was no actionable injury to the dominant owner's light, and had so reported. He was surprised, therefore, to be asked to come over to Ireland for the trial of the neighbour's action against the bank for loss of light, and begged to be excused. The solicitors, however, insisted and said that his presence would be a great comfort to the bank.

Came the day of the trial, and the plaintiff gave evidence, with much affecting detail, that 'Shure and your honour, don't I remember saying to Mrs Cassidy on May 9th how much darker it was than it had been on April 10th, and don't I remember the date well, because it was the very next day that Father Fitzpatrick himself came round to console me on the loss of me chickens' – or words to that effect. 'Would it make any difference to your evidence, Mrs Cadogan' (pronounced, for non-watchers of The Irish RM, Kay-duh-gawn, with the accent on the last syllable) asked counsel coldly, 'if I were to tell you that on May 9th the bank's old extension had been demolished, while construction of the new premises had not yet commenced?'

At this juncture, the judge tactfully rose for lunch, and my father plaintively enquired if he could go home now, since there was obviously no need for his services. 'I'm afraid not' said the solicitor. 'She's an auld widow woman and the judge is wanting to give her something.'

After lunch, the distinguished consultant from England gave his evidence, proving beyond doubt that there was no injury to the light, and the judge gave his verdict: judgment for Mrs Cadogan, and damages of £50. 'I see you were right,' said my father, 'but how could a poor old widow woman take the financial risk of such an action at law?' 'Well, isn't she a good customer of the bank, and weren't they supporting her?' replied the solicitor. 'Which bank?' my father asked, although he had already guessed the answer. 'Why, our clients, of course.' 'And what made you so sure she would win?' was the next question. 'Well you see' came the answer, 'some while ago she brought an action for breach of promise in this very court, and the same judge awarded her £50 damages. Her wily adversary, to avoid paying the money, married her instead and shortly afterwards decamped, so she really got neither her husband nor her damages.

Well, the judge was determined that someone was going to pay her £50, and it just turned out to be the bank.'

It can sometimes be advisable to know more than the mere words of a judgment before placing any great reliance on a precedent – especially an Irish one.

Index